INDIA(ISH)

MARK WALTERS

At the time of travel, ₹100 equalled £1 / €1.3 / $1.5

The f-word (as well as the c-word once or twice, though never the n-word) is used liberally through this book. And if you like yoga or knitting or *The Guardian*, or are the sort of person that orders a korma, you're probably going to hate it.

BODH GAYA TO GAYA

Buddha became enlightened beneath a banyan tree, and that famed tree is here in Bodh Gaya, the most sacred Buddhist site in the world. It's their Mecca, their Jerusalem.

The tree grows a metre from the pyramidal Mahabodhi Temple, which is adorned with hundreds of Buddha statues. Landscaped grounds surround the showpiece. Bowls of flower heads rest atop neatly tended hedges. Birds tweet, dogs snooze, squirrels scamper. A Garden of Eden feel, a serene peacefulness. On the lawns are monks: shaven-headed and robed in scarlet or orange; cross-legged in the lotus position, locked in meditation. At the side of the gardens is a large green pond, over and around which are strung hundreds of prayer flags; and in rooms at the rear are thousands of candles, each lit for a prayer.

Stone tablets state Buddhist teachings in different languages; one says: "Ageing in the peace and serenity of solitude, the learned joyfully reside in the forest as they leave their youth behind." It's apt for me as I'm ageing — today is my 33rd birthday — and I'm setting off alone to walk 1,000 km across India, which will likely include a lot of time in forests. Though it's not entirely appropriate, as it's debatable how learned I am, and this being India, I doubt I'll get much peace.

That walk starts from here, now; so I put on my flip-flops, having taken them off at the entrance, and walk out of the temple compound. Yes, I'll walk that 1,000 km in flip-flops.

The first stage of the trek is to a town called Gaya, 10 km away. I head there along a dusty two-lane road, flanked by a dried-up river on one side and rolling countryside on the other. The traffic is ceaseless. Thundering trucks, hurtling buses, careening cars, kamikaze motorcycles, plodding bullock carts, and wobbling bicycles compete for the racing line. I pass rustic villages of rudimentary dwellings — mostly round mud huts with thatch roofs. Women crouch outside them, cooking over open fires and washing clothes in buckets. Others roll cow dung mixed with straw into frisbee shapes and stick them on walls to dry. Ducks, goats, and cows wander; few are tied up or penned in. In one village, children play cricket with sticks and stones — a well-hit shot could break some bones. In another, two blokes stand next to a water pump; one works the pump while the other washes, covered in soapy suds. A shower is a two-man job here. I know what would happen if I called one of my mates to ask about that: "Hey Mike, can you come over to help me have a shower?"

"You're a twisted pervert. Don't ever call me again."

I pass chai stalls; at each, men — only men — sit on plastic stools, sipping sweet, milky chai from rough clay cups. Women, it seems, are too busy tending to children and working the fields to engage in idleness. At one stall, I come upon an unshaven stick-thin man with a phlegmy, hacking cough, who in between splutters rubs his teeth with a twig. He walks beside me and we exchange such pleasantries as his most basic grasp of English permits. When there's nothing else to say, for five minutes we continue in silence, until he turns off into a field.

After a few kilometres, I take a break at a bus stop and eat half a pack of Oreos. I like Indian food, but it's sensible not to test the steeliness of my stomach with an aloo masala rickaticka bongaloo curry when toilets are non-existent or in an awful state. Next to the bus stop is a barber shop in a mud hut. It's like a regular barbers in that there's a man with scissors stood in front of a mirror, cutting another man's hair; the mud hut is the only difference. Down the road, I see another barber so short on funds he can't even afford a mud hut. His mirror and shelf of hairdressing paraphernalia are nailed straight onto a tree.

Further on, a couple of dead dogs on the roadside. One is little more than a puppy — a dead one with its brains squished out. I'm full from my Oreo lunch, but there might come a time later on this trip that dead dog on tarmac becomes dinner. Dog meat tastes fine: I ate it twice when I lived in South Korea — once in a bowl of soup, once on the bone. Both times it was ordered for me in a group meal with locals, and to refuse would have been rude; it's not like I jumped my neighbour's fence, nicked their beloved Chihuahua, and put it in the microwave. There might also come a time that I become a dog's lunch: India has more than thirty million strays. (Bites from them account for around 35% of human rabies deaths worldwide.)

In Gaya, I pick a hotel at random. It's a typical Indian establishment: inexpensive, of dubious cleanliness, run by dirty-shirted blokes who shout and smoke and scratch their balls. Below is what the hotel advertises. (In brackets is the reality.)

Hot water (heat not included).

Daily cleaning (on Wednesdays).

Wifi (connection unavailable).

TV (old and broken).

Friendly staff (insert cash).

GAYA TO VARANASI

Packing doesn't take long because I have little with me — only 6 kg. I won't stay in one place more than a day or two, so no one will know I'm a skunky monkey who wears the same few items on repeat. For a couple of reasons, my clothes, flip-flops, and backpack are all black: filth and grime won't be so visible, and I don't want to be mistaken for one of those rainbow-shirted, baggy-panted muppets that frequent India. The snag is that I look like a shitty ninja.

My route from here is somewhat imprecise: westward towards the Taj Mahal. No set route means I can't get lost. (But if I find myself in Pakistan or Bangladesh, I'll admit that I am.) I can follow train tracks from Gaya to Varanasi — 250 km away — from where I can trail the Ganges River for 200 km to Allahabad. From there, I don't yet know. I'll deal with that when I get there — if I get there.

From a look at Google Maps when I last had wifi — and I should say at this point that I don't have a phone; only an iPod Touch — I know that the next town along the train tracks from Gaya is about 30 km away. I think I can walk that far in a day, though I haven't done so before, thus can't be sure. If I can't walk that far, I'll sleep outdoors; I'll slip into a bush at sunset. Should someone stumble across me, they'll be more scared than me; spooked at the sight of a ninja, they'll run off. Wild animals, however, don't fear ninjas. Leopards, wolves, and tigers are some of the man-eaters in these parts. But the risk is slight, and one I'll take.

I leave the hotel at 10 am, cross the road to the train station, go to the end of the platform, and walk along the tracks. A guard of dishonour has formed to see me off: people squatting either side of the tracks, blowing bum notes through arse trumpets. I'm tempted to do what people do when their puppy craps in the wrong place: rub their nose in it and smack their behind. That may be harsh, though: Hundreds of millions of Indians lack access to toilets and so have to poop al fresco. Besides, later it may be a case of pot, kettle, black as I join them in their open-air faeces fest. But I'll at least have the decency to go in a bush to do the deed. A different bush to the one I'll sleep in. The first rule of sleeping rough is not to shit and sleep in the same bush. Bear Grylls once did that on his TV show. What an amateur.

I leave the tracks for a series of rutted lanes parallel to them, fifty metres away; they take me through half a dozen villages. In each, I cause a commotion. Some stop me; others follow me. I'm asked the same few questions repeatedly: *Where going? What country? Your good name?* These repetitive conversations, interspersed with indecipherable head wobbles — part shake, part nod — are mentally draining. Every interaction is the same for me but novel for them. It's an insight into the life of a celebrity: badgered by people awed by my presence. But I smile, I chat; if they want a photo, I pose for it. Any perceived rudeness may turn them not just against myself but my whole country — and they already have reason enough for the latter.

A couple are unsavoury characters. I almost packed a knife and pepper spray in case of run-ins, but using weapons on locals in foreign lands is frowned upon — by everyone except NATO. So for self-defence I'm reliant on hand-to-hand combat skills learnt primarily from watching WWE. I've had a few fights before; results were mixed. I've sustained black eyes and bloody lips. My worst injury was a broken finger — incurred when I drunkenly punched a traffic light. There appear to be no traffic lights in India, so a repeat of that is unlikely.

After a couple of hours, I leave the village lanes to return to the train tracks, and progress is faster without the hassle. At Kastha station is a shaded bench between the tracks; I've earned a rest after walking 10 km. I unwrap a couple of samosas I bought at one of the villages. (I can't live on only Oreos; I'll get scurvy before I reach the Taj Mahal.)

I'm halfway through the first samosa when a guy in his twenties wearing tracksuit bottoms is on the scene — *Where going? What country? Your good name?* He wants me to follow him; to where I don't know. When I decline, he lingers and makes a phone call. After the call, he's even more insistent that I go with him and now keeps pointing at the station building that's twenty-five metres away. I tell him I'm not waiting for a train and don't need a ticket, but he doesn't understand. I decide the quickest solution is to go with him to the station and tell whoever's inside that I'm not waiting for a train. Then this guy has no reason to bother me any more and I can tell him to bugger off if he persists. So I go with Trackie Bottoms to the station — a cream-coloured, Victorian-era building with red arches out front.

Inside is a single room with a concrete floor and scuffed whitewashed walls. A precariously-hung overhead fan makes as much noise as a jet engine but generates as much breeze as a deflating balloon. At a cluttered mahogany desk is a pompous, spectacled, middle-aged man; his white, knitted jumper over his paunch makes him look like a sheep.

Sheepie — the station manager — gestures for me to sit on a plastic chair beside the desk. I give my set answers to the standard questions. But he has more English in his locker. He says, "If something unusual happens here, it is my job to report it, and you are, err ..."

"Unusual?"

"Yes."

I can't argue with that.

"You don't have permission to be here?" he asks.

"No, but do I need it? I'm just walking."

"Where are you walking to?"

He'll think I'm insane if I tell him the Taj Mahal, so I scale down my answer: "Varanasi."

"That is very far. It's too far to walk."

"But, you see, I'm writing a book about walking across India. So I have to *walk* to Varanasi, not take the train." I show him my notepad. "Look, writing a book." And I pretend to scribble in it.

He takes the notepad and flips through it. He tries to read some of the pages but can't because the hasty, untidy scrawls are unintelligible to anyone but me. He asks for my passport and phone. I hesitate but hand them over — my iPod Touch, anyway, as I don't have a phone. He inspects every page of my passport and asks Trackie Bottoms — who's been loitering throughout and must work here — to photograph the ID page and the page with my visa. He also asks him to take a picture of me.

Then Sheepie scrolls through all the photos on my iPod Touch. He pauses on certain ones — like the Nepal-India border crossing, roads and paths that I've walked in the last two days, and Gaya station that I passed through earlier. I also have photos of my written notes. Few of the photos are typical tourist ones.

Sheepie has eight telephones on his desk — none from the last couple of decades. He makes some calls; after the last one, he tells me I must wait here.

"Wait?" I say. "For what?"

"You must wait."

"For how long?"

"I'm not sure."

"Maybe I'll leave. You can't make me wait here."

"No. You can't go. You must wait."

"Wait for what?"

"You must wait."

I don't have to take orders from a train station manager, but to leave may cause unnecessary problems. He might call the police, and I don't want that. Better to leave on good terms.

Sheepie put my iPod Touch out of my reach. I ask him for it — if I have to wait, I'll at least listen to some music — but he says I can't have it. That's a bad sign, quite concerning; but when he later offers me tea and biscuits, I think, *Oh, this will be alright after all.* Then four khaki-uniformed, red-bereted, gun-toting soldiers walk through the door, and I think, *Bollocks; it bloody won't.*

Three stand guard by the door and one — evidently the chief — pulls up a chair in front of me. He talks — in Hindi — with Sheepie and then silently inspects me while he strokes his chin. Trying to work out, it seems, what I am. A foreigner who's been photographing infrastructure and writing coded notes. Yet I don't look like a spy or a terrorist. But neither do I look like a tourist. I'm an oddity, a queer conundrum. My passport and notepad are again perused, and there's another viewing of the photos on my iPod Touch. More pictures are taken of me.

Chief doesn't speak any English but asks me questions via Sheepie. He wants specifics: *where I've been in India, the dates I was at each location, which hotels I stayed at, how I travelled from place to place ...*

He thinks it strange that I entered India by land, not air. And he questions why although I have a visa, I don't have an entry stamp. My simple-but-unsatisfactory explanation is the border official didn't give me one.

Several phone calls next; five-minute babble sessions between Chief and Fuck-Knows-Who. The calls are punctuated with thirty-second pauses where he looks at me but says nothing. After the fifth call, I ask to use the toilet — a stone urinal ten metres from the station building. Chief agrees but sends a soldier with me.

After two hours with Chief, I sense the tide turning; sense that he's coming to the conclusion I'm not a terrorist, merely an idiot. But just as I think I'll soon be on my way, four more soldiers arrive. From the plethora of markings on his uniform, I know the Tom Selleck lookalike who leads this bunch is a superior of Chief. It's moved up the chain of command. The same process repeats: passport, notepad, iPod Touch, questions, phone calls. The difference is Selleck strokes his moustache instead of his chin.

I ask to get some fresh air after being in this room for five hours. Selleck sends two soldiers with me. I sit on a bench beside the station, surrounded tightly by a crowd of dozens of locals — who have been staring at me through the station door for hours. Heads at the back pop up like meerkats, angling for a better view of the caught animal. They jibber-jabber among themselves but speak not a word to me. I'm an exhibit; to be commented on, not interacted with.

After a while, Selleck comes out; he makes a gesture — follow him. Not back inside but to a white jeep parked behind the station. Selleck sits shotgun; I'm sandwiched in the back, a soldier on each side of me. At first, I don't know where we're going; then I recognise a village we pass: they're taking me back to Gaya.

The jeep stops outside a police station attached to the railway station. We get out and follow Selleck inside to a blue-walled, musty room. In the corner is a dungeon-like, dank cell; a couple of criminals grasp its bars. Ten or so police officers are in the room, sat at a long table; they drink tea as they fill in paperwork. None appear surprised at my arrival — I guess some of the phone calls from Kastha station were to here. Selleck speaks with a couple of the officers then leaves with his sidekicks.

I'm told to sit on a stool at the end of the table amid stacks of bundled paperwork. One of the cops writes a report based on my answers to his questions.

"Am I under arrest?" I ask.

"No."

"So I can leave soon?"

"You take train Varanasi. 9.15 pm."

"I don't want to take a train to Varanasi."

Another of the officers interjects, an older, authoritative-looking one. "You are taking train Varanasi. 9.15 pm it come. You get on it."

It's an order, not a suggestion. But I try to reason with him: "I'm tired. It's been a long day. I'll get a hotel in Gaya tonight."

"No. Train today."

"But—"

"Train today."

They haven't charged me with anything but also won't let me leave, even to go outside for a cigarette. They want me out of this state — Bihar — and into the next one — Uttar Pradesh (where Varanasi is). Then I'm no longer their problem.

I sit on the stool, silently considering my options. I realise I have only one: get on the train. They'll be pissed if I refuse. And if they're pissed, what will they do? Falsify a charge? Lock me up? I don't want to be in that cell in the corner, never mind a proper Indian prison. Maybe they wouldn't even *need* to falsify a charge. Possibly I *have* broken the law. Perhaps they're being generous in allowing me to go free, and I'd be a fool to do other than go.

At 8 pm, an officer says, "Come now. Earlier train."

I go with him through a door that leads directly onto the train platform, with two other officers flanking me. A blue train stretches along the platform, at least twenty carriages long; it looks like a cattle train with bars for windows instead of glass. I stand with my escorts while the other officer searches for the train manager, who he brings over to me. The train manager examines a document on his clipboard, then the five of us walk past several carriages before boarding one.

A foreigner boarding under police escort causes a stir in the carriage — stares, whispers, pointing. The leading officer tells me not to get off before Varanasi; then he speaks to the train manager — words I guess to be, "If he tries to get off before Varanasi, stop him and call us." The cops leave the train and wait on the platform, looking through the bars into where I'm sitting. Minutes later, the train departs.

In the sweat-stained clothes I've worn all day, I drift to sleep with a single thought on my socked mind: the epic walk is an epic fail.

VARANASI

I spent yesterday holed up in a hotel. I ordered room service aloo masala rickaticka bongaloo curries and watched a channel called Romedy Now. By my fourth romantic comedy, I'd rebooted and replanned: If I can't walk across India, I'll swim across. (A couple of rivers span its width.) But then I remembered that I haven't packed my Speedos. And the sizes stocked in shops here are too small to fit in my wang. Indians have todgers two inches shorter than Westerners' ones, a study found. I've seen the stubs of plenty of public pissers in India, and I confirm the results of the study.

So I can't walk, I can't swim. Buses and trains remain for what will be a full loop of India. Buses and trains don't sound as sexy as walking, and won't get me on the Discovery Channel, but perhaps it's for the best. Walking 1,000 km across India, I'd have seen only a sliver of the whole. Now I'll see the north, the south, the east, the west; a more comprehensive experience of the country, starting with Varanasi ...

A tangled network of hundreds of nameless and numberless alleys stretch from the river — the Ganges — that Varanasi straddles. They're claustrophobic and disorientating;

they're like an ant colony where the ants work not in unison and order but discord and chaos. Wardrobe-sized cavities line the sides of the alleys — vendors scrunch inside amid their wares: cloth and flowers, incense and carvings — and tucked in alcoves are candlelit shrines dedicated to strange-looking deities. Devotees go to shrine after shrine, pray to god after god, and clusters of red-arsed monkeys emanate menace, unperturbed by the tinkers, tailors, soldiers, dealers, holy men, poor men, beggar men, and thieves.

As I walk, I'm swarmed by scammers and spammers; they spout oily offers to go here or go there, to buy this or buy that. Like money-sucking leeches they attach themselves to me as I walk through the throngs. They're deaf to "no," so I use a Jedi-style hand wave to show "I'm not the foreigner you're looking for." One pushy dealer is particularly persistent. "Opium? LSD?" he says. Then he tries to palm a wrap of heroin into my hand. "Try some brown. Free!"

Beggars grab, plead, follow. "Milk, milk; no money, no money," cries a teenager who paws at me with one arm, cradles a baby in the other. And an urchin, about seven years old, stops me; she puts her hand to her mouth in an eating gesture. Before I shake her off — "Yeah, sorry, I would, but you know, I've been asked a lot already ..." — four more are with her. When I at last walk away, one clings to my arm and comes with me. It's a reverse abduction; against my will, I'm kidnapping a child.

Swear boxes would be more profitable than begging. With a ₹1 fine per curse, today they'd have made ₹100 from me. In India, I average an out loud for-fuck's-sake moment a dozen times an hour. I've already exceeded my annual swear quota — and it's only February.

Amid the chaos some calm: *sadhus* cross-legged, celestially-stoned; hair coils like snakes atop their heads and

Gandalf beards hang long and loose. Even a robe is too formal for some, who have only dusted themselves with ashes and tied a ribbon around their penis. They spend their days in pursuit of spirituality: yoga, blessings, meditation. And, for a price, posing for selfies with tourists — because ganja isn't free.

Cows, they roam free, stand and sleep where they wish. Even in the doorways of restaurants. They can sleep safely, for though India is a land of cows and curries, it's not one of beef curries. Cows are sacred to Hindus, to be exalted not eaten. In most of India it's illegal to kill a cow — do it and face up to ten years in jail. Vigilante groups "assist" the cops and are quick to act. Last year in this state — Uttar Pradesh — a Muslim accused of eating beef was lynched by a Hindu mob. (A police investigation later found that the meat was not beef but mutton.) While Hindus won't eat beef, they'll rinse a cow for the rest of its products. Milk, butter, and yoghurt are fair game. Some swig its piss, believe it purifies their soul.

Cows being everywhere isn't an issue for me; I do, though, have a problem with cowpats being everywhere. Flip-flops offer little protection against these organic landmines. "Argh, I've got shit on my foot," I mutter after I tread in one.

"It's holy shit," says a man near me. "It's good luck for you."

But holy shit still stinks of shit.

The shit fuses with the smells of decay and trash, sweat and smoke, and the resulting combination is a repulsive, reeking odour. Smoke swirls from hundreds of small fires smouldering — rubbish burning among a sea of the stuff. I'm part of the problem: after I don't see a bin for an hour, and realise I'm as likely to see one as I am a unicorn, I drop an empty bottle on the floor. Across India, in alley after alley, in street after street, is this carpet of garbage, and it's hard not to think that Indians are filthy fuckers ruining the planet. But are they? No. You and I are, in fact, filthier fuckers, more ruinous to the planet, as the average Westerner generates three times more waste than the typical Indian. The difference is that our waste is taken care of for us.

We recycle a lot less too. India has one of the world's highest rates of recycling — more than 50% of its waste. And I see now a couple of recyclers: barefooted and gloveless, sifting through a mound of garbage, scouring for recyclable scraps to place in their white sacks. This pair are some of the hundreds of thousands that eke an existence from the informal garbage economy, scavenging in rancid rubbish heaps, among the filth, the flies, the feral animals, risking infections and skin diseases. For ₹150 per day.

Down by the river, I see dead people. Not Bruce Willis having a paddle, but Indians engulfed in flames as their lifeless bodies lay on stacks of wood. Hindus believe Varanasi is a portal between the physical and spiritual worlds, and that dying and being cremated here provides liberation from the cycle of birth, death, rebirth. Bodies are burnt at one of Varanasi's eighty-plus *ghats* — chunky, stone steps that lead down to the river. The *ghats* stretch for seven kilometres against a backdrop of centuries-old Hindu temples and weathered residences. Corpses are cremated only at Manikarnika Ghat; other *ghats* are used for other purposes like worshipping or laundry or bathing.

I've no interest in watching bodies burn, but to see other *ghats*, I have to pass Manikarnika Ghat. As I pass it, a fifty-something bloke comes to me. "Here, come, look. Body burning now," he says through rotting, red-stained teeth.

I say I'm not interested, and I walk on. But he follows me: "You pay wood for poor families," he says.

I tell him no.

He says, "You come look at burning. You have to pay."

"I walked past the *ghat*, at the back of it. I'm not paying."

"Pay or problems for you. I make big problems."

"Go," I say, and wave him away.

"Pay me, then I go."

"I'm not paying."

I think: Why should I? You can't burn bodies in a public place and then complain if people see. If I barbecued my Grandma outside Marks & Spencer, passers-by would look at what I was up to. I wouldn't then ask them to chip in for charcoal.

"You think you smart, huh?" he says. "You will get beat. Go hospital."

He speaks with growls and hisses, and the ferocity of their delivery is disturbing. He looks not hard but wild, like a vicious weasel who would bite and scratch. Or throw acid: Last year, a Russian in Varanasi suffered severe burns after an Indian threw acid at her, and every year in India, there are hundreds of acid attacks.

He tries to hold my arm and tap my pocket, but I shrug him off and walk on. I've not stopped walking since he first spoke to me, and we're now a hundred metres past Manikarnika Ghat.

Still he follows. He says, "Give money now or more people come. And then you pay more. Make big scene. It very bad for you. You alone, we many. Look my eyes — this real."

I look at his eyes: I believe him — he's not messing around.

I could shove him, could smack his rabid face — stub this out before it spirals. But a crowd will form if I lose my cool, and who will they back? Him, I bet. A made-up story of the ignorant foreigner who disrespected their deceased brethren

— that's what they'll believe, not my tale that he's a malicious, scheming dickhead.

"How much?" I ask. (If it's tens of rupees, maybe for peace I should pay it.)

"₹1,000."

That's about a hundred samosas — screw that; that's a lot of samosas. And if I pay, he'll be motivated to repeat the scheme on other foreigners.

I tell him no and walk on. Still he follows.

A minute later, he speaks to a bloke we pass — another scoundrel; this one in his late-thirties — who jumps to his feet and follows along too.

The shit's so close to the fan that it's starting to spray. He has a straight flush; I don't even have a pair.

But wait, an opportunity, a previously unseen joker in the pack ...

I stop and feign that I'll pay, then abruptly charge down the steps of a *ghat* to a fella in a rowboat. I jump in. "Go, go, go."

We're off and away while the red-mouthed weasel is stood on the *ghat*, ranting and gesticulating.

"This man your friend?" the boatman asks me.

"No, that man's a motherfucker."

From out on the river, Manikarnika Ghat looks like the entrance to Mordor: blackened stonework, shrouded in smoke, a stench of death. The half-burnt bodies are dumped in the Ganges, but what really makes this river rank is the raw waste from the hundreds of millions of living beings that reside along its length from the western Himalayas to the Bay of Bengal. In Varanasi alone, it's reckoned the excrement of more than half the population — several million — flows unfiltered into the river. Tests on the putrid water showed up to 100,000,000 faecal coliforms per 100 ml — 150 times the safe level for bathing. It's revered, worshipped as a goddess; it's also a toxic sewer.

In the evening, I go to the station to catch an overnight train to Delhi. The scene outside resembles a refugee camp: bodies wrapped in crumpled blankets; gaunt, grimy people crouching, their butts hung an inch off the fetid floor. The blur of beings cough and belch and spit — a symphony of sounds, a concert no one wants to hear. I join the conveyer belt of bulging human cargo headed inside — warm bodies pressed too close for comfort; spicy sweat exchanged — and try to decipher the distorted announcements from loud-speakers that should have retired. Slouched against walls bruised with dirt are sunken-faced lepers gripping metal tins with their stumps — a hand-to-mouth existence without any hands. And on the platforms are people cooking and washing and sleeping; others have unpacked their bundles and bags. A lot look so at home that it's not clear if they're transiting through the station or living here, have opted to stay on after they missed their train. A train they came to get three years ago.

DELHI

Indians call Gandhi the Father of the Nation. Not for impregnating a record number of women — his tally totalled only one: a fourteen-year-old girl. (Calm down; he's not a nonce; he was only thirteen years old at the time.) The title was bestowed for masterminding the independence movement that secured India's freedom from Britain. *Satyagraha* was his strategy: non-violent civil disobedience — and his success influenced the Civil Rights Movement in the United States. He was a hero. Not everyone, however, agreed: Angry at him for opposing the partition of Pakistan and for expressing sympathy for Muslims, a Hindu assassinated Gandhi in 1948 — less than a year after India celebrated independence.

Gandhi's gone but far from forgotten. Across the country, roads and buildings bear his name, statues and portraits depict his form, and books and museums detail his life. Delhi's National Gandhi Museum is one such place. As I browse exhibits that chronicle how one bloke hassled an empire into submission, I'm approached by friendly Satish. "I'm here doing research for a new book about Gandhi," he says. "I work with Oxford and Harvard. I have received four letters from Queen Elizabeth about my books."

He thinks he's found a kindred spirit when I tell him I'm writing about India, and he wants to take me to libraries, museums, universities. "And you must come with me to the Mother Teresa Hospital tomorrow," he says. "I'm a volunteer. I talk to the patients and cut their nails. People there are very sick. Some have leprosy."

I say that it's more of a comedy book, that it will be light on history and culture.

He says, "So you are like Michael Palin?"

"Err, yeah, kind of," I lie, too embarrassed to tell him about the cock jokes and swearing and facetiousness.

From his bag he takes a sheet of paper that he hands to me; his CV, he says. It's mostly bullet-pointed statistics, and not what I expected for a writer like him. Highlights include:

"900 Books written."

"70,000 Songs written."

"110 Languages known."

"Gets up at 3 am."

He next shows me some letters he's received from luminaries:

"Mr Solanki, unfortunately, due to her busy schedule, the Queen is not able to read work that people send to her and provide a personal reply as requested. We thank you for sending it, however, ask that you do not continue to contact us on this matter again."

All are template letters sent by the minions of the Kings, Queens, and Prime Ministers he's spammed.

Satish guides me around the museum for an hour. For fifty-five minutes of this hour, he talks about himself. After, he insists that he walk me to Delhi railway station, near to where my hotel is. At the first road we have to cross, he grasps my hand. "Hold my hand," he says. "Drivers in Delhi are very dangerous." After we've crossed the road, I let my hand go limp, thinking it will prompt him to let go of it, but he either doesn't understand the hint or chooses to ignore it. We walk the next fifteen minutes hand in hand like we've come out a gay bar and are going home for some sexy time.

"See you tomorrow," he says as we part at the station. "God is great, and love is god."

I know it's a final farewell; he thinks it's only until tomorrow when we'll be at the hospital clipping lepers' nails.

I soon have another escort: Dressed like a sleazy porn star — with the odd exception of a sock over one hand — he flashes me a fake press pass then stalks me for ten minutes, squawking about taking me somewhere or other for something or other. He's a human vulture — one of the millions circling India — preying on naivety and politeness, confusion and tiredness. I give him the slip, but in fending him off, I've lost track of where I am, and in trying to shortcut a return to my hotel, I find myself in a maze of dingy alleyways of Dickensian squalor. Every step is on sodden, mangled garbage. Decrepit four-storey buildings, so compacted as to be claustrophobic, reduce the sky to a stroke of grey, and tangles of wires spread like a jungle canopy — stray ones dangle with the danger of snakes. Eyes in crowded, crooked doorways turn at me; inside echo the sounds of cramped dwellers, and I see silhouettes against flickering flames in shadowy rooms. Men size me up like I'm fresh meat in a prison. I feel the stares, sense the nudges, hear the mutters. No one smiles at me; not even the ragged, snot-nosed children. From the alleys sprout darker, narrower passageways; and at the end of each alley are only more alleys. I want out but weave deeper into the warren.

For half an hour I do this, until I see a bus pass the end of the alley I'm in: a bus means a main road, and a main road mean an exit — an exit from by far the most tragic area I've ever been in.

The main road, like most of Delhi, is tied in anarchic knots of traffic. Vehicles jackhammer through twenty-four consecutive rush hours in a million pneumatic blows. A traffic cop is stood at a junction resignedly waving about his hands; it's an ornamental position, simply for show. An umbrella can't stop an avalanche. Firm in the belief they need to reach their destination quicker than anyone else theirs, drivers seize an inch at the cost of a mile for everyone else. Autos (motorised rickshaws) are the worst offenders; driven like Panzers despite being tricycles powered by a lawnmower engine; they remind me of wasps: erratic, carrying a prick, annoying as fuck.

Cows, bicycles, rickshaws, and pedestrians wrangle with the cars and autos, buses and motorcycles. Pedestrians are the base of the pyramid and are dispensable. Traffic will swerve or slow for a cow but not a man. "Wanker!" I yell with alarming regularity as I dodge or sprint to avoid being mown down. I shout, I swear, I insult, though I know they can't hear my words through the tsunami of hardcore excreted from eight million horn-blaring vehicles jammed and enraged. Prolonged exposure to noise above eighty decibels, says the World Health Organisation, boosts stress hormones and causes hearing damage. Delhi is above that threshold consistently.

The noise pollution doesn't kill; the air pollution does. In parts of the city, airborne toxins are fifteen times the safe limit, suffocating residents, poisoning their lungs. As well as exhaust fumes: garbage fires, diesel generators, brick-making factories, coal-burning stations, construction projects. A bilious blend that makes locals cough and splutter. Delhians aren't alone in their suffering: four of the worst ten cities in the world for air pollution are in India, says the World Health Organisation. Delhi isn't one of those any more, but in 2015 was top of that list. Another study, the 2014 Environmental Preference Index, ranked India 174 out of 178 countries for air quality. The result is that air pollution is India's fifth-biggest killer — six-hundred thousand premature deaths a year.

Dirtied from a day in Delhi, the last thing I want to hear is there's no water at my hotel. There's a citywide shortage, says the receptionist, because protesters sabotaged a canal that supplies three-fifths of Delhi's water. The protestors are the Jats; their cause the opportunities available to their caste. They're not, however, a discriminated-against minority in Hinduism's infamous hierarchy. In the state the protest occurred — Haryana — the Jats are the dominant caste. It's an example of a curious, unedifying trend: mid-to-upper-level castes competing to be classified as "backwards". The winners of this race to the bottom receive access to the government's affirmative-action programme, which guarantees reserved quotas for university admissions and government jobs.

The religious-rooted caste system assigns every Indian one of four castes at birth based on the caste of their parents: Brahmin, Kshatriya, Vaishya, or Shudra. Brahmins, it says in the scripture, emerged from the head of Brahma, the Hindu god of creation; Kshatriyas from his arms; Vaishyas from his thighs; Shudras from his feet. Outside those castes are Dalits (formerly "Untouchables") — who, I assume, got shat from Brahma's arsehole. The four castes are further divided into more than twenty thousand sub-castes. The one an Indian is tagged with influences every aspect of their life, from social status to vocation to marriage. For those in the upper eche-lons of the hierarchy, the system is perfect; meanwhile, those at the bottom are locked in a rigid social order they can't climb.

To one Indian I said the UK's class system doesn't sound all that different from the Indian caste one, with northern working class monkeys downtrodden by southern middle and upper class fairies. He said, "But in the UK, the son of a potter can study, can go to university; he can be a doctor, a lawyer, a politician. In India, that is rare. In India, the son of a potter will almost certainly be a potter."

The caste system is less harshly applied than it was, but prejudice remains widespread. Dalits in particular — 15% of the population — are kept on the margins of society. In a 2014 survey, a quarter of Indians admitted they refused to socialise with Dalits — or even eat beside them. The discrimination they receive from their countrymen is far worse than any Indian abroad may have to deal with. A Dalit sunbathing on Bondi Beach wouldn't get his *lungi* in a twist if called a curry-stinking cow-shagger.

Few Dalits will make it to Sydney, though, or even Colombo for a city break, because they're given only the worst-of-the-worst lowest-paid jobs — cleaning the toilets, sweeping the streets, and the like. Given only shit work to do, others see them only doing shit work, think they're only capable of doing shit work, so keep giving them only shit work to do. And so on goes the vicious, shitty circle, on and on and on.

———

Delhi is one of the most densely populated cities in the world, with more than ten thousand people per square kilometre — exceeding double that of New York or Tokyo. Of the twenty-five-plus million that live here, a minority are behind closed doors; most are on the street: buying or selling, shouting or honking, pissing or eating. The pandemonium is of a nature seen only at a particular place and time in the UK: Primark on Black Friday.

Delhi has no Primarks, few brand name shops at all. Rupees are mostly spent at one-man enterprises. Floor mat to pushcart to wooden stall to alcove shop to actual shop: these are the stages of an Indian business. (Many max out at stage one.) The wheels of the upper stages are oiled by blokes who pace the streets with heavy loads on their heads, transporting goods between businesses, making deliveries to customers. Their cargo ranges from cement to HD TVs to gas canisters to cuddly toys. They do the job of a van driver despite not owning a van. 85% of India's workforce are part of this off-the-books economy, which partly explains why less than 3% of Indians pay income tax. If 85% of the workforce each paid 3% tax, the government would have enough rupees to install not only a toilet in every Indian home but a bidet too.

The nut-seller sat on an upturned bucket, a dozen small packs of nuts laid in front of him on a cardboard box, is an example of stage one. An entrepreneur at stage two is the guy sat atop a pushcart of socks; he's shoeless so as to model a dark-green, cotton pair. He's not an ideal model, isn't as impactful as the mannequins in Victoria's Secret. He does make a sale, though, to a one-legged fellow with a walking stick. Two legs are generally preferable but only the one has its perks: each pair of socks bought lasts twice as long.

Paan is often sold at stages three and four: wooden stalls and alcove shops. A mild narcotic made from areca nut and wrapped in betel leaf, *paan* is chewed for a light buzz. Chewed but not swallowed. The streets are stained with the blood-red juice that's spat out, gobbed through reddened, rotted teeth — the odious outcome of long-term use. *Gutka* is a synthetic, mass-produced alternative sold at every mom-and-pop shop. It's sold in packs similar in colour and size to sachets of shampoo, and foreigners sometimes, I suspect, confuse the two: try to wash their hair with *gutka* or chew shampoo.

Also keen for rupees are beggars — "Sir, ₹10, give me. ₹10, sir. ₹10!" On Delhi's kerbs and corners in their thousands — amid scabbed, skeletal strays, agitated by the bedlam — they lift their bowls and give the sad eyes they've practised nine-to-five for years — maybe decades. One, who has only one eye, stares at me; I stare back, and it turns into a competition: first one to blink loses. I tell myself: If he wins, I'll give him ₹10. I blink first but don't pay him as it wasn't — I reason now — a fair contest: With an extra eye, I had twice as much chance of losing.

I leave the crush of commerce to enter a park, at the entrance of which a man in his twenties — quiff-haired and wearing a leather jacket — says to me, "I have sex with you, please."

"Err, no," I say, before adding, "Thank you," to match his politeness in saying please.

Less polite is his pursuit of me around the park. In Indian eyes, he's a criminal: not for stalking but because homosexuality has been illegal in India since 2013 — after a brief spell from 2009 when rimming and felching were legal. With fudge nudging outlawed, it's odd to see in India so many men holding other men's hands — a far more common sight than a man holding a woman's hand. Factor in half of Indian blokes wearing sheets around their waist instead of trousers, and you have the absurdity of it being the norm in ultra-prudish India for two men in skirts to prance around hand in hand.

Indian women aren't so brazen. It's been so long since I've seen a woman's legs or shoulders that I've forgotten what they look like. They're not so modest with their midriff. Some would be better hidden — *wobble*, *wobble*, *wobble*. Chubsters are, however, a minority: based on BMI, around 20% of Indians are overweight; 40% are underweight.

The density of people in Delhi — even if many are stick-thin — makes it necessary to compete for space. Nowhere more than on Delhi's metro, where en route to the Akshardham Temple I'm rubbed and groped more than a baby-faced choirboy at St Patrick's Cathedral. To elude the frotteurs, I may buy a sari so I can use the women-only carriages. Indian women with facial hair aren't uncommon, so I wouldn't even need to shave. I saw a woman with a full-on beard board a women-only carriage. She was either India's roughest woman or India's laziest transsexual. The dowry for marriage — paid in India by the bride's family to the groom's — would be six figures. (Pounds, not rupees.)

Not all women can fit in the women-only carriages, so must brave it in the mixed ones. Signs in these carriages publicise the "Delhi police helpline for women in distress". Shiva help any woman who must rely on that ...

"Hello, this is officer Bhardwaj at Delhi police station. How can I be of assistance?"

"A man is harassing me."

"Ok, what are you wearing?"

"You mean what is *he* wearing?"

"No, what are *you* wearing?"

"Err, a blue sari."

"And what colour underwear? Or no underwear? You saucy minx."

One sign warns that travelling on the roof of the train is punishable with a ₹50 fine; others instruct people not to sit on the floor and warn of a ₹200 fine for spitting. Some still spit; some still sit on the floor.

Built of pink stone and white marble, the palatial

Akshardham Temple features 9 domes, 234 carved pillars, and over 20,000 hand-sculpted figures. It's at least as impressive as the Taj; in my opinion, more so. It sits in manicured grounds and is surrounded by a lake into which water is routinely added from 150 of India's holiest rivers. The water is first filtered, it seems, as in the lake are no turds or charred pinkies.

The temple is a tribute to Bhagwan Swaminarayan, believed by his followers to have been a god. Within is a gold statue of him beside murals that depict his life. Aged eleven, he began a bollock-naked seven-year pilgrimage on foot across India. Prudently bypassing train tracks meant he wasn't forced aboard a train on the second day. With seven years of starkers sauntering under his non-existent belt, he amassed a fan club of hundreds of thousands. Aware that mixing fame with nudity makes for tabloid headlines, he started wearing clothes — including wooden flip-flops, a pair of which are on display. Not shoes, not trainers, not high heels, but flip-flops. Gods wear flip-flops — I rest my case.

At night, I board a bus bound for Rishikesh — eight hours away. Above the seats are sleeper berths; I've treated myself to the latter, and I'm smug as I climb above the seat paupers to my bed, chuffed to have a restful night of horizontal snoozing ahead of me. Five minutes later, a middle-aged bloke climbs up to join me. I tell him he's got the wrong bed, that this one is mine. But he shows me his ticket, and I'm hit with a terrible realisation: this is a double bed, not a single. For fuck's sake. Spooned through the night by a man I've only just met: this must be how an Indian bride feels on her wedding night. I insert my earphones and close my eyes — try to pretend he's not there. But I can feel his warmth, smell his odour. I might piss the bed to see if it forces him out. From the look of the mattress, I wouldn't be the first to have tried this.

RISHIKESH

Within the shitcake I've been eating, Rishikesh is a sweet, glazed cherry. Nestled in the forested foothills of the Himalayas, the Ganges bisects the town, and flows fresh from the mountains, free of faeces and corpses. On its banks, bells ring and chants float from ancient, colourful temples; ensconced within are *sadhus* and pilgrims, praying and prostrating, searching for salvation.

It's famed for being the cradle of yoga. Now hippie types flock to the town, the faithful and the freaks shopping in India's spiritualism supermarket. They join the locals meditating and contorting beside the sacred river. The guys try very, very hard; to impress the ladies, I suspect, because there are no bars or clubs in this town. Being able to perform a flawless Macarena under the influence of a dozen Jagerbombs holds no sway here. Unless a guy can touch his toes — without bending his knees — and talk about *kundalini* for fifteen minutes, he has no chance of getting laid.

Around town, every shop and cafe has included a New Age word in their name — Freedom or Babylon or Krishna. Pinned to noticeboards inside are headshots of people purporting to be masters but who are patently muppets. The services advertised are manifold: reiki healing, tarot readings, trilotherapy sessions, consciousness maps, spiritual awakening — to name only a few. The one offering, "A journey into the time tunnel through soul molecule activation to appear in different time-space realities of human history," isn't a joke.

I had thought to spend a week in one of Rishikesh's many ashrams, places where you live a monk-like existence and spend all day doing yoga and meditating and sweeping floors. They're part fat camp — for people who have piled on mental rather than physical weight — and part cult, where you bare your spiritual hole for a bearded bloke to poke. It turns out, however, that International Yoga Week is next week, and so all the ashrams are booked up with people perfecting their postures and poses. But I'll still get my yogic groove on via some drop-in classes.

I've never tried yoga, but I may be a yoga person who just doesn't yet know it. I like tofu, I like whales, I like sitting down — the signs are there. I decided I'd need yoga pants and went to a shop earlier for that purpose, but when there I couldn't go through with buying some. I tried a few on, looked in the mirror, and thought I looked ridiculous. Every pair was so misshapen that even Krusty the Clown would deem them too ludicrous. So I'll attend the classes wearing jeans; the only jeans I have: skinny black ones.

The classes I've signed up for are at the Himalayan Yoga Retreat, which has a studio with a glass wall that looks out onto the Ganges flowing down from the Himalayas. The first class is Pranayama, a type of breath yoga that incorporates chanting. The instructor, Swami Prakash, looks like Jesus — if Jesus was Indian and sponsored by Tango. Only one other attendee, who resembles Thierry Henry in his Arsenal prime.

Swami and Thierry have some rapport; he's evidently a regular attendee.

We sit cross-legged on yoga mats; me beside Thierry and Swami facing us, a couple of metres away. Swami mumbles something I don't catch because of bells ringing outside, and then they both, with eyes closed, start a ten-second-long, synchronised, "*Ommmmmmmmm.*" I join in on the second and subsequent rounds of it. My voice range doesn't go very deep: They're doing Stevie Wonder "*Ommmmmmmmms*", while mine are more Bee Gees: "*Ommmmmmmmmm*, staying alive, staying alive, *ommmmmmmmmm*, staying alive, staying alive."

After some sitting in silence, Swami says we'll do a some-thing-or-other chant. "I haven't got a printout to give you," he tells me. "Just listen and try to join in when you think you've got it." I listen intently to the random sounds they make, none of which are recognisable as words. It's on par with singing karaoke in Chinese. I keep quiet most of the time but chuck in the odd "uh" or "ah" now and again to let them know I'm still involved.

We do some breathing equivalents of rubbing our stomach while patting our head, then move on to something else I don't catch the name of: I have to rest my left hand on my knee and adopt a Trekkie gesture with the right, which I use to block one nostril while inhaling through the other. "Slower, slower," Swami tells me, as I hoover up air as one would a line of cocaine.

The next class — Hatha Yoga — starts straight after the first has ended. Three more people join us — looking-the-part twenty-somethings who will one day have kids with names like Peace or Sky. For five minutes, we sit with our knees floored and our bodies angled back over our bent toes. It's supposed to be a comfortable relaxation posture, but my knee joints are in pain. I'm grimacing; everyone else is smiling.

What follows is a super intense session of what is effectively a game of Simon Says ...

"Simon says lay on your front, with your hands in front of you, and arch your back."

"Simon says put your legs apart, with both heels on the floor, and bend low to your right side."

"Simon says put your right foot in front of your head, your left foot behind your back, and flap your arms like a chicken."

The kid in PE class at school who had no hope, like the lard-arse running cross-country, or the wheelchair boy doing the high jump, today I am him. If it weren't for my earnest, pained face, Swami would think I'm taking the piss.

"Your heel isn't on the floor," he says. "Get your bottom down ... What's that hand doing there? ... No, *over*, not under ... Keep your mouth closed ... You're *inhaling*, not exhaling ..."

My ears are working; I know what I should be doing. It's the rest of me that's not working. My body just won't bend that way or that far. It's not my fault — it's genetics: my Dad has had both knees and hips replaced. I'm built from shoddy materials.

Swami eventually concedes that I'm as much a lost cause as a eunuch attempting the Kama Sutra. He starts giving me separate instructions to everyone else: "Everyone do x, y, z. Except you," and he points at me. "You just stand there and put your hands on your head."

Next comes pairwork exercises, and I get paired with Thierry. We lock limbs and push and pull each other; the result is something between a UFC match and recreations of erotic Italian sculptures. Thierry is, of course, better at the exercises than me. I'm complicating what would otherwise be easy for him. We're like Siamese twins, where one is in good shape but has an extra head and random limbs awkwardly attached.

When Swami tells us to take a rest, I assume it's the halfway point. I lay there looking like Stephen Hawking, wishing I'd prepared a contingency plan for this, as a debacle was always on the cards considering I haven't even jogged since 2014. If only I'd forged a note from my Mum saying I need to leave early for a doctors appointment. Shiva shows mercy on me, though: it's the end of the class.

It would be wrong of me to say yoga is a sham, nothing more than a ploy to shift excess stock of clown pants after the demise of circuses. I tried my best, but it wasn't a fair test on the merits of the practice. The test needs to be redone by someone more flexible than a plank of wood.

After a few hours interlude, I return to the scene of my yoga crime for something which should be simple: a class on meditation and mindfulness. Swami arrives ten minutes late; he says he forgot there was a class at this time. I don't know how much confidence I can have in a mindfulness teacher forgetting about his own class on mindfulness.

No one else has come for the class, so I'm one-on-one with him. After we sit, he starts with a warning: "You must know that meditating can bring up feelings of misery, despair, loneliness."

I think: That might explain the one-man attendance.

He says we'll work through some techniques he developed during a several-month stint in a cave in the snowy Himalayas. He has me huffing and puffing, moving my chin up and down, and adopting peculiar positions with my arms.

For the last technique, he tells me to lay on my back with bent knees and make a noise that sounds like "shoe" on every inhale and a "ha" noise on every exhale: "Shoe haaaaaaa, shoe haaaaaaa, shoe haaaaaaa ..." He leaves the room while I do this, and I lay there alone for fifteen minutes keeping it up: "Shoe haaaaaaa, shoe haaaaaaa, shoe haaaaaaa ..."

When he comes back — by which time I can "shoe haaaaaaa" like a pro — he tells me to stop and lay there quietly with my eyes closed. As I lay there, I feel a warmth that starts in my toes rise slowly up through my body. I think: This malarky actually works: I'm a believer!

Then he says it's the end of the class and to open my eyes, and I open them to see he's put a portable heater by my feet.

In the evening, I attend a talk by a guru — Shri Prashant — at the Tree House Ganga Cafe. Three times today, I've been given flyers for the talk. The flyers declare Shri Prashant the founder of the Advait Movement and make a couple of bold claims: "The purpose of Advait is for the creation of a new humanity through intelligent spirituality." And: "His unique spiritual literature is on a par with the highest words that mankind has ever known."

The room the talk is held in is made from bamboo and wicker. Shri Prashant sits at the front on a cushion throne. He wears a yellow scarf and tracksuit bottoms and woolly socks. His appearance and demeanour are that of a baddie in *Scooby-Doo*; one who plots for world domination but is scuppered by meddling kids and their dumb dog. He's very precise about how the room is set up: no one can sit on a chair and no one can sit next to anyone they know — and he also says all phones have to be handed in and that we can't leave until the end. One guy walks out on hearing he can't have a chair. Everyone else — about thirty of us — sits on mats in a compact semi-circle around Shri Prashant.

He has half a dozen assistants. They were the ones handing out flyers earlier, and now they scurry about as per his commands. He gets them to give out double-sided A4 sheets printed with Bible teachings. He asks us to read the handouts, and then he sets about roasting Jesus, picking holes in the teachings. "Don't focus on the prophets of the past," he says. "Those like Jesus come and go. You need to be open to new prophets and know that they may have a different appearance to previous ones. Open your eyes; you're missing what's in front of you."

What he says over the next hour is wishy-washy; spiritual-sounding but lacking structure and specifics. If someone questions his nonsense, he closes them down and tells them they don't understand, that they're "scared of the truth". But many in the room have glazed expressions and hang off his every word. Some make notes — me too. I worry Shri Prashant will see me writing and ask me to share my thoughts. I don't want to read aloud that I've written I think he looks like a villain from *Scooby-Doo*.

Ninety minutes in — and by now a few have walked out — Shri Prashant goes nuclear: "I'm not going to sugar coat it. The people closest to you are those who will prevent your progress along the path. Do not stay attached to the false family of mother or father, brother or sister, husband or wife. They lead you astray from the truth. Leave them all behind for a new dynamic family. It is the only way for your salvation."

He eases off a bit after this with some random tangents, including five minutes on how squirrels live and what we can learn from their squirrelly ways. I mostly agree with his thoughts on squirrels.

I want to stick around to the end of the talk to catch the final hard sell and maybe get a free keyring, but my brain cracks three hours in after a twenty-minute back-and-forth about using the word "gain" in a spiritual context. I spring to my feet and make a dash for it.

Having Shri Prashant as my only Facebook friend would put a stop to endless baby photos in my feed, but I can't justify ditching everyone I know for a bloke that I share some common ground with regarding squirrels.

He's not the only one in town with a messiah complex. I've seen many wannabe messiahs here — both Indians and foreigners — walking around barefooted with feral hair flowing over their baggy tunics. They must be kept apart; friction is inevitable when they meet ...

"I'm the messiah."

"No, *I'm* the messiah. *You're* just a long-haired chump who can't afford shoes."

"Your mum's a long-haired chump who can't afford shoes."

"I have no mum. I was sent to earth by Brahma."

"Then who's that woman with the same surname as you who's the only one that follows you on Twitter?"

"Screw you, Dave."

"I'm not Dave; I'm Davarius."

"Your name's Dave, and you're a dickhead."

Fisticuffs follow; some scratching, a bit of hair pulling. Then they part; one to yoga class, the other to the time tunnel.

MCLEOD GANJ

McLeod Ganj sits two thousand metres up in the Himalayas. Its mist-soaked ridges and valleys are steep and thick with pine trees, and buildings are tacked onto the slopes like magnets on a fridge. No snow here but visible in the distance are the white-clad peaks of the stark-faced Dhauladhar mountain range.

I arrived here after fifteen hours on an overnight bus from Rishikesh. I chose a seat instead of a bed to sidestep the roulette wheel of a sleeping partner — the odds favoured Mashni from Mumbai over Stephanie from Stockholm. I didn't have to share my seat. I'd have gone ballistic if for fifteen hours Mashni had to sit on my lap. Sleep was minimal despite a seat of my own: The bus lurched and thumped through the night as we corkscrewed our way along mountain roads twisting intestinally. Headlights picked out glimpses of eroded banks, and barriers irregularly bordered the roads — a token gesture, they would have stopped nothing but a skateboard.

It's famous for one thing, this town: being the home of the Dalai Lama. When China invaded Tibet in 1959 and forced him to flee, India granted asylum. They offered McLeod Ganj as a base for the exiled Tibetan government and as a refuge for Tibetans escaping oppression. India giving the Dalai Lama sanctuary is one of the reasons China and India aren't on friendly terms. The border between the two has long been closed. Before thinking it's incredibly generous of India to give McLeod Ganj to the Tibetans, first consider a couple of points: it's statistically the wettest place in the country, and an earthquake in 1905 led to it being all but abandoned. India only let them have it because they didn't want it anyway. They deserve some credit, though, as there would be a national meltdown in the UK if it were announced a whole town were to be given to refugees — pitchforks and torches come out if three pizzerias open within a three-kilometre radius.

15,000 Tibetan exiles have joined His Holiness in McLeod Ganj — that's three-quarters of the population. The number would be higher, but it's a perilous journey from Tibet to here, harsh conditions through mountains patrolled by the Chinese army, and Tibetans caught escaping are punished severely. These refugees have transformed this once-empty settlement. Tibetan monks sit in circles discussing the Dharma. Tibetan temples, schools, libraries, and workshops flank the narrow, sloping streets. Stalls sell Tibetan accessories — beads, scarves, incense, statues, charms ... — and cafes serve Tibetan staples: buttermilk tea and plates of steamed dumplings. There's little to suggest anything of India. McLeod Ganj isn't, though, a Tibetan paradise. These people are displaced — they don't want to be here. It isn't a home from home but an interim solution; a critically important improvisation that bottles the culture the Chinese are erasing in Tibet.

In shops and hotels and restaurants, framed photos of the Dalai Lama hang. I already knew what he looked like as I've seen him on TV before — giving speeches at United Nations conferences and chucking eggs at Chinese-looking people in Toronto and Perth — but despite knowing what he looks like, I could have unwittingly passed him a dozen times today as his distinctive appearance in a Western setting — a bit chubby, a shaved head, maroon robes — is what most of the monks here look like. Realistically, though, the chances are the Dalai Lama is out of town, because while McLeod Ganj is his official home, he's not often here. He says he's off promoting Buddhism and the Tibetan cause, but if you tickled him on the issue, the truth would come out: he's on constant holidays because he lives in a shitty house on a steep hill.

His house is in the Tsuglagkhang Complex, along with the Tibetan government and a museum and a temple. A well-worn path — the Kora Circuit — surrounds the compound, which crowns one of the highest ridges of the town. Monks and pilgrims use the path for walking meditation, repeatedly circling it like a roundabout of religiosity. The path is lined with colourful prayer flags tied to barbed wire fences, and is dotted with brightly-painted, drum-shaped prayer wheels, each inscribed with thousands of mantras. The temple — the largest Tibetan temple outside Tibet — is on the topmost terrace of the complex. Like the rest of the site, it's not fancy nor flashy. It reminds me of a school assembly hall. Through its open doors, I glimpse a gilded Buddha statue; before it, on the wooden floor, pilgrims kneel in fervent prayer. Present are monks not only from Tibet but also India and the West. Some sit meditatively, rubbing prayer beads between thumb and forefinger; others circle the outer walls of the temple, rotating the prayer wheels lining its sides. A few perform prostrations: they stand with hands clasped before dropping to their knees and stretching their body out flat; they then stand again to repeat the process. Again and again and again — for hours at a time.

Outside the museum are a monument and display dedicated to the 138 self-immolations in Tibet since 2009, carried out in protest against the occupation. They soaked themselves in flammable liquids then set themselves alight; as the flames consumed them, they shouted slogans demanding freedom for Tibet and the return of the Dalai Lama. Some Tibetans feel — in the face of worldwide apathy — that this most desperate of measures is necessary. That the initial invasion happened a half-century ago means to most people around the world that the event has been relegated to the history books. This is a mistake: It's very much of the now; this very day China are actively oppressing Tibetans and exterminating their culture and values. We look back at tyrannical takeovers of the past and ask why no one stepped up and did anything about them; well, it's not too late for Tibet — something can still be done.

Diplomacy isn't the solution — that avenue has been exhausted. And China is too big and too powerful for military leverage to be viable — the Dalai Lama's failed egging campaign is proof of that. They'll only listen if their pockets are affected, which will only happen by boycotting Chinese-made products:

- Don't eat noodles. (Pot Noodles are made in Wales, so are ok.)
- Drink Tibetan buttermilk tea instead of Chinese tea. (This is harder than it sounds: buttermilk tea is rank.)
- Refuse to upgrade your iPhone. (They're manufactured in China, not an elf-run production line in Steve Jobs's garage.)

- Stop looking at pandas in zoos. (They're native to China and the zoo likely imported them from there. I know they're cute, but sacrifices must be made.)

McLeod Ganj can be walked from end to end in fifteen minutes, and that's not far enough to stomp off my anger about the chow-meiners refusing to get out of Tibet, so I head out of town up a slanting road towards the surrounding mountain meadows. Colourful houses, many quite grand-looking, spread across the landscape; some are leftover from McLeod Ganj's time as a British hill station in the nineteenth century. It doesn't take long for the irony to hit: I'm walking around an ex-British hill station — from where the former oppressors governed their stolen land — to let off steam about the Chinese occupying Tibet. The British ruled India for almost two centuries; China has spent barely a quarter of that in Tibet. Perhaps I should be angrier at my ancestors than the Chinese.

Apologists say the British gave India democracy, gave English as a unifying language, gave a railway network ... The summary: India today would be an even sorrier place without British intervention. But there's no doubt that Britain governed for the benefit of Britain, not India — no empire ever pursued predominantly altruistic policies. Britain earned themselves a fortune: India was their empire's most profitable cash cow. So any benefits India received during that time were really funded by themselves. To say Britain was charitable, to congratulate Britain for anything they gave, would be like thanking a mugger after he rinsed you of £50 then gave you back £2 for your bus fare.

Britain, it seems, felt guilty: for many years after they left India, the country was the biggest recipient of British overseas aid. That guilt recently subsided: British aid to India officially stopped on the 1st of January 2016, with politicians saying, "You're doing missions to Mars? You've got more billionaires than we have? Well, that's the end of that. No more pocket money for you." Indians aren't bothered: Britain gave £200 million a year, compared to the £70 billion a year India itself spends on welfare. India's finance minister undiplomatically dismissed Britain's aid as "a peanut".

Worried that cussing the Chinese makes me a historical hypocrite, I let them off the hook and instead enjoy the vividly-flowered landscape. For a couple of hours, I follow an ill-defined path, my mind and senses bathing in the all-too-rare space, silence, solitude. It's the most pleasant of my daily walks from recent weeks, in which I've averaged eight kilometres per day. Most of those kilometres have been a pedestrian's nightmare. I stuck to the scuffed, uneven pavements where I could, and ventured onto the holey roads where I came upon an insurmountable impediment or the pavement inexplicably disappeared.

At least half the pavement has been unwalkable. Common obstacles forcing me into the road include parked motorcycles, advertising boards, makeshift homes, restaurant tables, rubbish mounds, electrical boxes, sleeping people, feasting cows, food stands, shop wares, tree trunks, brick walls, sand piles, chai stalls ... Then there are the bowled balls and leprous limbs and phlegm projectiles — and a thousand other inbound hazards to contend with. Jumping and dodging and ducking are par for the course. Simply walking — normally an autopilot activity — is in India an extreme sport.

MCLEOD GANJ TO
AMRITSAR

I'm taking a stop-at-every-town, unreserved-seat bus to Pathankot (90 km away); then a second such bus for 120 km to Amritsar. The seats are soon filled and aisle packing begins. Indians aren't discouraged by an overcrowded bus — they never decide to wait for the next one — and bus conductors display powers of Biblical proportions by finding slithers of space where before there were none for the miraculously multiplying numbers.

While on the whole awful, these buses aren't without merit: they're really cheap (about ₹150 per 100 km) and they've got sliding windows — the type banned by health-and-safety sticklers in most countries because they think people can't be trusted not to lose their head to passing vehicles. (I think if the cost of some breeze on a bus is a dozen decapitations a year, it's a fair price to pay.) An A4 printout of a compass is stuck to the front window of this bus — a poor man's GPS. I'm not sure if a 3D printer can make a usable compass, but a 2D one 100% can't. That's not the only comical thing stuck on the window: there's also a list of names and phone numbers, and the second name on the list is Dikshit. If my name were Dikshit Walters, this book would be published under a pseudonym.

The guy sat next to me — I see out the corner of my eye — is Googling "sexiest kiss videos". Getting aroused on a bus is totally unacceptable. The filthy bastard. In the toilet on a plane for a flight longer than three hours: we all accept that, we've all done that. But a bus? No. And a bus you've been on less than fifteen minutes? Fucking wrong. I think this bloke sees that I've clocked what he's up to as he stops scrolling through the videos and searches for "news" instead — or maybe he's just hoping today's news is "Exclusive: Angela Merkel Shares Sexy Kiss With Vladimir Putin." When that guy gets off the bus, I gesture to a woman in the aisle that she should take the seat. She gives me the type of look given by the hottest woman in a club to the most pissed bloke in it who's just tried to grind with her, and opts to stand next to the empty seat rather than sit next to me. Another woman turns down the seat too; she prefers to squeeze in on a seat with two other people. I feel like a paedo sat on the swings at the park. I think a rumour has spread that there's a guy on the bus watching sexy kiss videos, and I've been falsely fingered as the bus wanker.

A few hours into the journey, the bus weaves along two-lane roads through a landscape of farms and fields, hills and villages, under a sun that beams in a clear blue sky. Life in the land, life in the people — life blooming, not clinging on. Women work the flush fields, harvest the watery soil — their bright saris like exotic flowers. Others carry vessels on their head, walk down dirt paths past scarecrows made from bin bags and wooden crosses. Buffaloes wallow in muddy ponds; oxen pull crude ploughs guided by blokes brandishing whipping sticks. Goat-herders and river-bathers are others in the frame of what could be a watercolour of Indian life from a century ago.

Scenes like these are why I prefer taking buses to trains. The speed being slower, more of the surroundings are absorbed, appreciated. Via a stream of transient tableaus unfolding onto the window canvas, they provide an excellent vantage point from which to observe Indian life.

The colours of the buildings and vehicles and clothes in these passed-through scenes are of the like seen on your TV when you've let your Nan have the remote and she's gotten confused and started button bashing: over-the-top oranges, yowser yellows, garish greens, piercing pinks, rasping reds. Signs for shops and restaurants supplement the wackiness; though they're typically hand-painted, they're like WordArt on steroids: combinations of effects like 3D and warp and emboss used on fonts like Comic Sans and Brush Script and Papyrus. That everything looks cartoonish is no bad thing. Life should be more like a cartoon, less like a documentary.

A staple in every fleeting diorama are slowly-stirred large pots — specialities concocted day in, day out, for years going on decades — and metre-long stalks of sugar cane being squeezed into mangles from a past age. In go the stalks, out drips pure sugary goodness. Seen less frequently are butcher shops, but there are more than you might think for a country that has more vegetarians than the rest of the world put together. Only 40% of Indians are vegetarian, though, which means there are seven-hundred million who still need their meat fix. Few Indian butchers have refrigerators, so must slaughter on demand. That slaughtering takes place in plain view, with bloody-handed butchers in blood-stained shirts standing in the street, clutching knives and carcasses like deranged serial killers. Behind them, from iron hooks attached to the ceilings of their stuffy shacks, dangle disembowelled and beheaded goats. Beside them are live goats, tied in a line to a rope, awaiting their grim fate.

At Pathankot, by the entrance to the station's toilet, a guy in his mid-twenties, with a 'tache and a baseball cap on backwards, is sat on a chair behind a table. Such a man is common: to collect the few rupees charge for using the loo. On my way out, I hand him a ₹10 note. He smiles and holds out his hand to shake. The handshake goes on too long, and he starts rubbing the palm of my hand with his thumb. When he at last lets go of my hand, he points at me, then circles his finger around his face. "Face nice," he says.

"Thanks."

"Su ..., su ..."

"Uh?"

"Su ..., Su ..."

"Super? You're too kind," I say, guessing that he's adding a second adjective to the compliment.

He starts sucking his little finger and moving it in and out of his mouth; then, with his other hand, he thumbs towards the nearest cubicle.

"Oh — suck-suck?" I say.

"Yes, suck-suck. I suck-suck you."

Maybe he doesn't have change, so is offering ₹7 worth of blow job in lieu of ₹7 in cash.

"No, thanks," I say. "No suck-suck for me. Keep the change."

He looks disappointed when I walk off.

Perhaps it wasn't about the ₹7: It's a dull job; he may just have been looking to pass a bit of time. But I was bored working at Marks & Spencer (which I did for four years when I was a student) and never once offered blowjobs. It would have been frowned upon — especially as I sometimes worked in the childrenswear department.

Close by, a man stands next to a cart laden with piles of nuts. "₹50 — Mix?" he asks.

"Yeah, sure," I tell him.

He makes a little bag out of an old sheet of newspaper and grabs and drops fists full of nuts into it. I hope his hands are cleaner than his shirt. What's on those fingers could be the worst of the worst: According to India's Public Health Association, only 53% of Indians wash their hands with soap after defecating, and only 30% before preparing food. And this in a country where bog roll is as rare as bins. As for those eating, only 38% were found to wash their hands with soap before a meal. Food is nearly always eaten with fingers in India, so what that 38% put in their mouth could contain two flavours of faeces: their own and the seller's.

As well as food being tainted with turd, it's laced with stray hairs. I've found more hairs in my food in the last month than I have during my previous 396 months combined. Back in the UK, I'll have to go to a vet to get a giant hairball removed. I can offset the vet fees by selling the hairball to a bald Indian in Birmingham, who will be pleased to get his hands on a wig of natural hair from his motherland.

Near to the nut-seller is a drinking establishment for the common Indian man: a squat, concrete building with a Kingfisher (the logo of India's most popular brand of beer) painted on the side. Inside is a caged counter containing shadowy shelves of booze, dealt out by a hairy man wearing a holey vest. A few plastic tables and chairs, over which hangs a naked light bulb. The tables are covered with empty bottles and cigarette ash; the floor with spittle, vomit, litter. Outside the bar, a man a couple of metres from the entrance writhes on the floor, sick around his mouth, his *lungi* soaked through with piss. A few metres further on, in the gutter between the pavement and the road, two other guys lay; one uses the kerb as a pillow, and the other his friend's leg. Such a sight isn't rare, and outside off-licences queues are often lengthy and disorderly. More Indians drink than you might suppose for a super-religious country. In only four states is alcohol prohibited. The other twenty-five states amply cover for those teetotalers: 1.5 billion litres of whisky alone is drank in India every year.

A scramble to board the next bus, and I'm as bad as the others, elbowing and shoving to secure a seat. My gentlemanly manners have ebbed away in India; they've had to for me to survive. Whenever I've been courteous — like letting someone board first or holding a door open — nine times out of ten, they haven't smiled or nodded their thanks but blanked me or looked at me like I'm a wimp. Even without being a gentleman — and despite my size advantage — I'm rarely one of the first to board. Women are as bad as the men and can't half shove when they need to. One stamps on my toe today, and I'm sure it isn't an accident.

The bus pulls over a few minutes after setting off. I poke my head out the window to see why and see the driver stood feeding pigeons. The other passengers seem fine about this. As we ride into the Punjab, the turban count — which has thus far been low on my travels in India — accelerates. The Punjab is the land of the Sikhs, and to honour god's gift of hair they won't let a barber near their barnet. Not having a haircut since childhood naturally results in a Rapunzel-like appearance, hence the bulging turban to keep it in check. For the most devout, the hair-cutting embargo extends beyond only head hair: the beards on show make Hagrid seem clean-shaven. And there's a reason why you never see a Sikh sport Speedos.

By the time we pull into Amritsar, I've clocked an eight-hour shift on buses, only going 210 km in the process. Some may see that as a day lost, but I've been tuned into India for the duration of it; the sights and sounds and smells sparking my senses. To see the real India, you need days like this.

AMRITSAR

Amritsar is to Sikhs what Liverpool is to Scousers: the most sacred city in the world, unsurpassable in its supremeness — despite substantial evidence to the contrary.

The city's Golden Temple is their Anfield. Pure gold plates the shimmering structure, intricately engraved with motifs and inlaid with precious stones; and a holy pool surrounds it on all sides, ringed by a rectangular walkway made of gleaming white marble. The queue to enter the inner sanctum is as long as the Ganges. Those in line are keen to see the Guru Granth Sahib, Sikhism's holiest book — and have a sing-song too: the book contains poems and hymns which are sung non-stop through the day.

Those not in the queue are walking barefooted around the pool, or kneel in prayer on the walkway, or sit and lounge, enjoying the vibes, the tunes: strong beats with melodic vocals and silvery percussion. Some strip to their pants and immerse themselves in the water, said — though as yet only as scientifically proven as homoeopathy — to have healing powers. You'd think those wading in would wear their best pants for the occasion, but they mostly haven't; well-worn y-fronts are the common choice — white ones. (The problem with white is that when wet it becomes see-through.)

Everyone takes photos. Indians seldom smile for theirs. They adopt the look of someone trying to work out 857,264 divided by 153. One man asks a foreign woman for a photo. She refuses. His friend points out me: I smile, start to fix my hair. The man shakes his head. But a woman with a baby is keen; she hands me the baby, wants a picture of me holding him. I feel obliged to comply even though I don't like holding babies: I worry about an ill-timed sneeze, that I'll drop them. Still, it's better she's taking my photo with her baby than her giving me her iPhone and asking me to photograph her baby and her. If I drop her iPhone, it'll cost me ₹40,000 to replace it. But if I drop her baby, I can replace it for free with one of those abandoned on the streets outside.

The Golden Temple is as peaceful as can be today, but it's endured some dark days. In 1984, the prime minister — Indira Gandhi — ordered special forces to attack the temple, where militants demanding an independent homeland for Sikhs were holed up. Many were killed in the raid, and the temple was damaged. Sikhs worldwide were pissed off. Revenge was had four months later when Indira Gandhi was assassinated by her bodyguards. The bodyguards were Sikhs — someone in HR dropped a bollock there.

Even darker: In 1919, the British opened fire on peaceful, unarmed protestors in the garden beside the Golden Temple. More than 1,500 wounded or killed. The locals won't have forgotten about that, so if anyone asks where I'm from, I'll say Spain. People often mistake me for a Spaniard anyway — maybe the way I walk makes me look like I'm doing flamenco. Not knowing any Spanish is a hindrance, but I can wing it by saying the names of Spanish football players with generic foreign noises mixed in: "*Ah, no Englishe. El Fabregas uh Casillas. Ole, ole Iniesta eh ah Ramos Ramos.*" I've used this pseudo-Spanish manoeuvre in nightclubs to fend off trolls. Only one time did it fail: the Shrek turned out to be a Spanish football aficionado and asked why I was listing the Spanish national team. I got out of that pickle by deftly switching to French football players.

While the Golden Temple is a serene oasis, a sanctuary of order and cleanliness, the usual India chaos and filth span out beyond its marble entrances through dirty, noisy streets pungent with the reeking aroma of trash and piss. If even half of the loving attentiveness on display inside India's temples were exerted outside them, India would be one of the world's most attractive countries, rather than one of its most minging.

That swathes of India have been spoiled and scarred in part explains why many Indians have left: sixteen million have emigrated to one place or another in the world — that's more than the individual populations of more than a hundred of the world's countries. Much of the damage and defacement can be put down to there simply being too many Indians: nearly 20% of the world's population on 2.5% of the world's landmass. And that's now: the population is set to double by 2050.

China's one-child policy took a lot of flack, but was it such a bad idea? If I were prime minister of India, I would implement a similar policy. Fewer people facilitates the reduction of disease, poverty, illiteracy, malnutrition, and a massive bunch of other issues that India struggles with. Issues largely dealt with in China.

With Amritsar being a dive, I take a bus to Wagah, 30 km away. Through Wagah runs the Radcliffe Line that marks the border between India and Pakistan. After the 1947 agreement to partition Pakistan from India, British lawyer Cyril Radcliffe had only five weeks to draw the line. Five weeks isn't a long time, especially for someone — like Radcliffe — who hadn't been to India before and had no border-making experience. It was thus hastily and arbitrarily drawn. Neither side was happy with it, and it lead to chaos, violence, bloodshed. In the years since the acrimonious divorce, the India-Pakistan border has remained a throbbing wound. It has plagued relations between the neighbours, resulting in four wars: 1947, 1965, 1971, 1999. The situation is calmer than before but tempers remain frayed. Wagah is the only legal crossing between the countries, and it's heavily militarised.

While I've mulled an early exit from India, I'm not coming to Wagah to cross into Pakistan — talk about out of the frying pan into the fire. I'm here because every day, just before sunset, the in-conflict countries have a showdown at a ceremony that marks the nightly closing of the border. Soldiers section the crowd — numbering in the thousands — into two lines: one for men, one for women. In a first for India, the queues are orderly. IDs are checked, and bodies are patted; then we file through a kilometre of barriers and roadblocks and checkpoints, past the barrels of machine guns peeking over sandbags.

A road stretches from this side of the border, through an imposing gate, to Pakistan. A couple of grandstands border the road on this side; both are rammed, a kaleidoscope of colour. Indian flags are waved and there are singalongs to beat-pumping *bhangra*. It's full-on fever pitch. Beyond the border gate, about fifty metres away, Pakistan's grandstands are visible. Men sit in one, women in the other; both are only a quarter full. Everyone is sitting; no one cheers. Gloomy Islamic wailing is just about audible. The contrast to the

Indian side is as stark as between a funeral and an eighteenth birthday party. Clad in a white tracksuit, the Indian MC encourages clapping and dancing, general frivolity. He asks women to come down from the stands to the road; dozens do so. Nose rings and necklaces and amulets groove to the tunes: head wobbles, shoulder shimmies, finger twirls, pelvic thrusts, toe spins.

Once the women have returned to the stands, a military drummer begins to pound a beat. On both sides of the border, half a dozen built-like-a-brick-shithouse soldiers take up position on the road, ten metres from the gate. India's wear khaki uniforms and red-fanned turbans; Pakistan's, black uniforms and black-fanned turbans. A stone-faced Indian soldier steps up to a microphone, inhales deeply, then bellows a prolonged "*Aaaaaaargh*". At the same time, on the other side of the gate, a Pakistani thunders back: "*Aaaaaaargh*". It's a scream-off — to see who's the loudest and longest. There's no clear winner. They're both excellent at screaming.

The two soldiers then set off on a brisk goose-stepping march to the gate, closely followed by their barrel-chested, moustachioed companions, each glaring menacingly at the rivals coming straight at them. Based on India and Pakistan's turbulent history, you might assume what happens next is a shoot-out; but no, it's a dance-off. At the gate, they come to a halt, and the lead fellas engage in a sequence of synchronised, intricate stomps and high kicks with all the pizazz of Michael Jackson. One gets *too* into it and nearly knees himself in the nose. Their moves done, they end with a long-held death stare.

For twenty minutes this battle-ballet goes on, with each of the soldiers having a chance to shine in a one-on-one. Officially, the result is a draw, but in my opinion, India trounced Pakistan.

The ceremony concludes with the lowering of each nation's flag — done at the same time. Then comes the first and last physical contact between the rivals: a brusque handshake.

As the gate is being closed, I shout over: "You're just a shit India, shit Indiaaaaa, you're just a shit Indiaaaaaaaaaa."

AMRITSAR TO BIKANER

99% of buses in India range in quality from shite to god-damn-fucking-shite. Despite this, the drivers live out F1 dreams in them. Several times today I've cursed and braced, an imminent untimely demise seemingly inevitable as the bus I'm on sped straight at oncoming vehicles at law-busting speed. No seat belts, of course; divine protection is cheaper.

Their size means trucks and buses rule the roost. Outfitted like Mardi Gras floats, but roaring and snorting and growling like incensed hellhounds, they spew toxic black fumes from their rear, red jets of *paan* from their sides. Their horns cease-lessly sound off like vexed war cries and issue wrathful intent to all, challenging anyone to a duel to the death. Between them, suicidal motorcyclists weave, while autos compete like kamikaze dodgems.

Drivers of all vehicles are always trying to pass. Even when traffic in the other lane is doing likewise; even when the vehicle in front is moving faster than them. The only time they back out from a manoeuvre is the second before a head-on collision with a vehicle larger than their own, when they violently swerve back into their lane. Some fatally mistime that last-second swerve, as evidenced by the skeletons of deceased vehicles lining the road.

Crudely-made skull-and-crossbones signage labels some stretches of road as hotspots for accidents. Around the world, this would signal caution, and people would reduce their speed; the typical Indian driver, though, will accelerate on seeing such a sign. My guess is they think the less time they spend in an accident zone, the lower the chance of having an accident. There's some logic in that reasoning, but not enough to result in less accidents: 150,000 die annually on India's roads, and a further 500,000 are injured, making these roads among the world's most dangerous.

As well as twatty driving and terribly-maintained roads, an excess of vehicles is to blame: in the past decade, the number of vehicles on Indian roads increased two-hundred-fold, while the total length of road networks increased only eight-fold. Ultimately, though, fault rests with the drivers; lots of whom literally shouldn't be driving. One set of official data that looked at 180 million driving licences found that an estimated 50 million were bogus. The law isn't much help: the penalty for using a fake licence is a measly ₹500 fine.

Not long after passing one accident zone sign, the bus slows to swerve around a man flat out in the road, pools of blood spread around his head. No vehicles have stopped, no one has run to his aid. He may have a long wait: In a national survey, three-quarters of respondents said they would be unlikely to assist a road victim with serious injuries. And it may be an hour or more until a paramedic arrives at the scene. A study by the *Indian Journal of Surgery* found that 80% of road accident victims in India don't receive any emergency medical care within the first hour after an accident. In many regions, ambulances are simply too few; in larger cities, those there are get delayed by traffic. 50% of the fatalities, the study said, could be averted if victims were admitted to hospital within that first hour.

After four hours, I arrive in Bathinda. Feeling my luck on roads is waning, I opt for a train for the next leg of the lengthy journey to Jaisalmer. India's trains are safer than its buses but by no means safe: 25,000 a year die on its railway network. Some of those deaths are probably murders occurring at station queues for tickets. Each queue resembles an angry mob, but the queuers are irate at one another, not a common enemy. Ferocious is an understatement. It's no holds barred, and eye-gouging is fair game. I get into testy argy-bargy with one guy who tries queue-jumping me when I'm about to be served. Stares and shoves exchanged. I've never before seen someone be so pissed off with someone they're pushing in front of.

My ticket from here to Bikaner, 300 km away, costs ₹110. That's for the bare basics option — Unreserved Second Class — which is all that's left. It doesn't guarantee me a seat; if I get one, it will be on a shared bench. The other options for long-distance trains are AC 2-Tier, AC 3-Tier, Sleeper. Few trains have a First Class carriage. AC 2-Tier is how I travelled from Varanasi to Delhi. There were ten sets of six berths in the carriage; each berth had a padded bench that doubled up as a bed. Clean sheets and a pillow were provided; a cooling breeze blew from overhead air conditioning. AC 3-Tier is the same as AC 2-Tier except there are 30% more beds squeezed into each carriage. Sleeper has the same amount of beds per carriage as AC 3-Tier, but there's no air conditioning, and no sheets or pillow are provided.

I find a bench on the platform and settle in for a three-hour wait. Trains of twenty-plus carriages come and go, just some of the 12,000 plying the 65,000 kilometres of track that embroiders India, easing the ebb and flow of a billion beings seemingly forever on the move. Every time a train comes, the waiting crowd morphs into a mosh pit. Before the train even stops, a Darwinian scramble to board ensues. Included in this survival of the fittest are those trying to disembark, who incur the penalty of an enforced journey to the next station for not being fit enough.

An hour into my wait, a man sidles up to me on the bench; he looks like an Indian Robin Williams who's spent a month on the streets. He's eager to chat, but there's a missing language connection, and after an hour of awkward incoherence, we're none the wiser about each other. Sensing a second such hour ahead, I hand sign that I'm going to the toilet, thinking I'll sit at the other end of the platform afterwards to get some peace. My plan fails: he stalks me to the toilet, shadows me at the urinal, then tails me to the new bench.

From a comparison of tickets, it turns out we're waiting for the same train. Soon after he knows this, he offers me a masala peanut. I don't want one — definitely not this one, held with fingers so mucky that I can see the dirt. Another tick in the no-fucking-way-am-I-eating-that tally are the tales of food-spiked druggings on Indian trains to rape and rob.

I gesture that I don't fancy it, but he persists.

Do I — A — cause offence by resolutely refusing?

Or — B — take it, pop it in my mouth?

I take it, eat it. I had to — any traveller worth their salt knows there was really no choice.

To counter possible malicious intentions, I give him one of the stray US dollar notes in my bag. It may earn me mercy from any evil plan he has — surely he wouldn't poke a gift horse up the arse.

When my train comes, Mucky Fingers takes my arm and drags me aboard. He wrestles us some space on a couple of benches among a group of guys — scruffy-looking; in their twenties — and some middle-class sari-wearers. Each vinyl-covered bench is meant for three; we have five on ours. (And two guys are laid out in luggage racks above.) The back of the bench isn't padded at all; the seat of it only slightly. The fans aren't switched on, and the windows aren't open. A sticky cocktail of spicy body odour lingers.

The lack of space means I can only get one arse-cheek grounded at a time, and from the little of the bench my buttocks can touch, a pneumatic paddling results as the train non-stop rattles and judders. If only I had a bit more fat on my bony behind. I once saw a documentary about Brazilian women getting bottom implants and I thought, Yeah, I might give that a try. I don't want a sexy Latino butt, just a bit of cushioning. Legroom is also scarce. The distance between the benches — which face each other — is less than that for a single seat on a UK train. This minimal gap has to accommodate twenty legs. Whenever someone goes or comes back from the toilet, a game of leg Tetris breaks out.

The aisle is in constant motion: toilet-goers, drink-sellers, snack-touters. "*Chai, chai, chai,*" or "*Pani, pani, pani,*" or "*Biriyani, biriyani, biriyani,*" are rhythmically called by men traipsing through with pots and buckets and canteens, offering seat delivery in place of a non-existent restaurant carriage. I'm not deviating from Mountain Dew and dry biscuits, hoping dietary restrictions keep me from using the squat toilets in carriage-wobbling conditions. I hope we hit bumps in the track when the biriyani-eaters are squatting, and the karma for devouring stinky food in an enclosed space is toppling backside first down into the abyss.

I mentally nickname the guys near me: Judge, Scrawny,

Indie, Lazy Eye, Sleeps. They're my kind of people; the sort of guys I'd talk to on a train in the UK — if talking to others on UK trains wasn't a criminal offence. Judge says he and Scrawny are on the way home from a friend's wedding — a fifteen-hour journey from their hometown. If I received an invitation to a wedding that necessitated a booty-busting thirty-hour round trip on a train as packed as Gandhi's Independence Day Bhangrathon and as reeky as the little man's post-jive loincloth, the RSVP with "Regretfully Decline" ticked, circled, and underlined would be sent by courier within the hour.

"You money, how much get?" asks Lazy Eye at one point.

Word of my salary spreads around the carriage. Everyone is astonished, even though I purposely reduced the figure as low as I thought I could realistically get away with. That I'm unmarried also works its way around; it astounds people even more than my salary. Pitying looks come my way.

My iPod Touch draws attention, gets passed around. Its contents are pored through, including all my photos. Soon my earphones have been in half a dozen ears, and my bottle of Mountain Dew the same number of mouths. That's the way it works on Indian trains and buses: what's yours is mine, and what's mine is yours. The personal becomes the public.

Within a couple of hours, bonds have been built: Indie rests a hand on my leg, Scrawny offers to lend me his blanket, and Sleeps is snoring with his head on my shoulder. Judge even invites me to go with him to stay at his house in Jodhpur. My ache-afflicted arse bones prevent me accepting the offer — they can't hack the additional six hours it would take to get there. Even Mucky Fingers turned out alright; he's been giving me regular smiles and nods. I feel guilty now for earlier thinking he might have roofied me. (I'll continue double-dosing nicotine gum, though, just in case.)

These guys have undone the work of hundreds who have begged and cheated and badgered and connived over the past weeks. There have been days I've felt this country is more of a cuntry. Today isn't one of them.

BIKANER TO JAISALMER

Through the bus window is yet another India, wholly different to what I've seen so far ...

Lonely figures trudge across a shimmering, sun-bleached expanse of dry plains strewn with spiky acacia bushes. Camels roam with cows and goats, picking wearily through the dusty stubble. In every direction, a vast emptiness that goes on and on.

Sometimes I need to remind myself I'm still in the same country. Bodh Gaya and McLeod Ganj, Delhi and here: each contrast to such a degree they could almost be in four different corners of the world. I am indeed still in India, though, and still only in the far north of the country.

Something that hasn't changed across the places are the keen starers giving me long, lingering, documentary-length looks. I came as a spectator but find myself a spectacle, constantly under innocent yet intense scrutiny. The contingent on this bus, possibly bored of the unvaried scenery, are the gawking goggle-eyed worst yet. I don't understand the drawn-out fascination. I'm just a man sat on a bus, doing nothing. What I'm doing right now is the same as what I was doing five minutes ago, and is what I'll be doing for each of the next five minutes. What are they expecting me to do? Start juggling? Unzip and windmill? Spontaneously combust? I've been known to watch live streams of *Big Brother*, though, so perhaps I'm a hypocrite.

After an all-too-long-and-awkward while, the guys in the aisle stood nearest to me — the most diligent rubberneckers — start taking turns for the seat next to me. It becomes a meet-and-greet of the like seen at Z-list celebrity book-signing events. One will sit down and shake my hand, and we'll exchange a few words using whatever English he can muster from his school days. He'll then snap a selfie with me and shake my hand again, before vacating the seat for the next guy.

Every day this carousel of conversation occurs, flicking my nerves, tapping my brain. I find myself saying a lot, yet nothing of note; generic waffle the locals force out of me.

This is a genuine conversation I've had:

"Name?"

"Mark."

"Age?"

"Thirty-three."

"District?"

"District? You mean country?"

"District."

"Birmingham."

"Sister?"

"Yes, one."

"Sister's job?"

"Advertising."

"Sister's district?"

"Birmingham."

"Cousin name?"

"Which cousin?"

"Yes, cousin."

The attention I attract is 99.99% of the time from men. The scales of forwardness are off-balance: Indian men are too forward, Indian women not forward enough. To be expected, perhaps, for India is a man's world.

For starters, men have a numbers advantage. As of the 2011 census, there were only 940 Indian women for every 1,000 men. The global average is 984 women for every 1,000 men. The numbers are skewed further for children up to six years old: 914 females for every 1,000 males. This gender imbalance is one of the most pronounced in the world. Where are these missing women and girls? In many cases, suppressed before they were even born. Tests to determine a foetus's sex are illegal in India; however, they're still available — sometimes quite literally under the counter. If the test shows the baby's going to be a little Anaya instead of a little Aarav, a coat hanger is inserted.

The principal reason for the high rate of aborted female foetuses is a daughter being considered a financial liability, compared to a son being an asset. As well as a daughter having lower earning potential, parents will have to pay a wedding dowry to her future husband's family. Dowries, although illegal, are still commonplace. The cost more often than not totals hundreds of thousands of rupees, plus possible add-ons like refrigerators, motorcycles, televisions. For poorer families, even the ₹30,000 for a PS4 alone may put them in debt.

Once married off — probably as a teenager, to someone she didn't choose for herself — the norm is for a woman to live with her husband's family, where she'll have to do all the household chores under the command of her mother-in-law. If she puts too much chilli in her husband's curry, or accidentally scratches his *Call of Duty* disc, or — god forbid — fails to give birth to a son, a beating may come. More than a third of married Indian women have suffered physical abuse at the hands of their husband. The worst-case scenario is atrocious: burnt alive. The extreme practice of dousing a woman in flammable liquid and setting her alight still happens. In 2013, the National Crime Records Bureau figures reported 8,083 burnings — nearly one every hour.

Doing a midnight runner from a demonic family of in-laws is for a few reasons problematic: her own family may shun her for sullying their reputation; as a divorced woman, she'll be seen as damaged goods; and if she's not well-educated, she'll struggle to support herself. The chances are she won't be well-educated: one-third of Indian women aren't even literate (compared to one-fifth of Indian men). This has a knock-on effect on the type of work women can do. Of the women working in India, more than two-thirds do so in the agricultural sector. Mostly as labourers, mostly for a pittance.

Another problem for Indian women is the threat of sexual assault and rape. The reported incidence of rape has risen over 50% in the last ten years. And it's believed only a small percentage of attacks are reported. The reluctance to report a rape or sexual assault is due in no small part to the woman feeling she will be blamed for the incident. She may be deemed at fault if she was out on her own or wearing "inappropriate" clothing. Should a rape case make it to court, it results in a conviction only a quarter of the time. If it's marital rape, the case will never make it to court. Indian law states: "Sexual intercourse by a man with his own wife, the wife not being under fifteen years of age, is not rape."

Considering what Indian women have to contend with, it's no surprise that a 2012 Reuters poll of 370 gender specialists ranked India as the worst place to be a woman out of all the

G20 countries. And a 2011 Reuters report — contributed to by 213 experts from five continents — ranked India as one of the top five most dangerous countries in the world to be a woman.

I get a particle of insight into what Indian women have to deal with when a guy takes the spare seat next to me and after some back and forth for fifteen minutes — in which he whispers that he's gay and tells me of the difficulty that entails in India — squeezes my leg and says I'm "lean". Five minutes after that, he asks, "Do you like boys?"

"No," I say.

Whenever I try and veer the conversation to something else, he barges it back to his favoured theme: gayness. Then he drops the batty bomb: "Can I touch your dick?"

"No."

A few minutes pass.

"I don't mean inside your pants. Just like this ..." He rubs his little finger over his crotch.

"No."

A few more minutes tick by.

"Go on," he says.

"No."

He brushes my leg with his hand. I knock it away.

"I think you're scared," he says.

He's using reverse psychology 101 to try and worm his way to a feel of my willy.

"No, mate. I'm not scared. I'm just not gay. But, that aside, we're on a bus — a fucking bus."

"Oh, if you don't want to do it on a bus, we can get off and go somewhere private."

"No."

Until he leaves the bus — a full hour later — we sit in awkward silence.

If that's what women in India have to deal with on a daily

basis, they have my sympathies. A bus ride in India is uncomfortable enough without strangers trying to fondle your sexy parts.

Six hours after leaving Bikaner, I reach Pokhran and have to change buses. As is standard at Indian bus stations, it's a hubbub hive of activity. Dull, achy throbs radiate from rattling buses crowded beyond capacity, groaning under the weight of excess passengers and their excess luggage. The conductors for each stand by their wheeled deathtraps blowing whistles and yelling — and yelling is no exaggeration — the destination for their bus: "JAISALMEEEEEEEEEER." Chai-sellers stand boiling sweet tea in vessels over the hissing blue flames of gas stoves. Two blind beggars with bowls collide, and a teenager air-bowls to practice his technique — hanging on to dreams of being the next cricket superstar despite the extreme likelihood that he's destined to peddle or pour his way through life. Ornamented women outfitted in saris and shawls and veils jangle from their ears, noses, necks, wrists, feet. Little girls holding tin pots knock the sides of buses as they move in vain along the open windows. A woman with a sack of cement on her head leads four small children behind her, each carrying a ham-fisted homemade shovel on their shoulder — *heigh-ho, heigh-ho, it's off to work they go ...*

My seatmate on the bus to Jaisalmer has tics; he sniffs and grunts non-stop. The schoolgirl sat in front turns around and can't decide which of us to stare at. She eventually settles on him. I feel strangely jealous but don't resort to grunting and sniffing too to try to win her over. I should be a gracious loser, let him have his time in the limelight. The bassy-voiced troglodyte sat a couple of rows behind breaks out in song; a third of the bus follows her lead. *Oh, a song, that's nice. Oh, another song, how lovely. Oh, a third song, what a surprise.* Fast forward through two more hours of songs and I've turned into

Simon Cowell, facepalming and shouting, "It's a no from me. A big, fat fuck-off no."

When we reach Jaisalmer, a motorcycle with two guys on it pulls parallel with the still-moving bus. The one riding pillion peers through the open windows one by one. When he sees me, he holds up a sheet of paper with "Welcome Mark" written on it. This is odd: I haven't booked any accommodation.

"You spoke with my friend at Pokhran," he says through the window. "You buy Mountain Dew from him. I'm here to meet you. He told me you needed a hotel in Jaisalmer. I will take you to my place."

The crafty bugger. He's using what I thought was polite small talk over a Mountain Dew purchase at Pokhran to hassle me in Jaisalmer before the bus has even stopped.

I say, "Mark? No, I'm Gordon."

He knows I'm lying. It can't be mistaken identity: I'm the only foreigner on the bus.

"But ... you're Mark," he says. "You *must* be Mark."

"No, sorry mate. Not me. I'm Gordon. I drink Coke, not Mountain Dew."

He gives up the chase. A score for ~~Mark~~ — I mean Gordon — versus the scheming touts.

In my hotel room, the first thing I do is drop my pants in front of the full-length mirror. Today's bus ride bumps and thumps have worsened the state of my already ruined rear-end. The damage: two bruises, one on each cheek. If anyone sees my bruised buttocks, they won't believe my explanation. Dominatrix spanking, they'll presume; public transport is too implausible.

JAISALMER

Jaisalmer is a city in a desert with an ancient fortress; a place I couldn't miss, even though its location way out in India's north-western bulge is inconvenient. It's an outpost, alone near the frontier; like Newcastle, but with more sand, fewer Geordies, and naughtier neighbours than Scotland.

The hassle of getting here is made worth it on sight of its monumental sandstone fortress sat on a rocky mound that elevates it from the vast desolate desert vista all around. It could be a fairytale sandcastle; it's almost mirage-like in appearance, an illusion conjured by the Psammead. Though nine-hundred years old, its imposing ramparts, circular bastions, and crenellated towers look as solid as ever. An army of twenty thousand goose-stepping, screaming Pakistanis, doing the full repertoire of moves from *Saturday Night Fever*, could spin and shake and shuffle for a year and still not breach it. All the buildings within, as well as most of those outside, are the same colour, all cut from the same sandy cloth. Shops and cafes and hotels flank its snakey lanes and steep stairways; plenty of homes too, for the thousands who call the fort home. Yet modern life hasn't spoilt this survivor of the past. It retains a medieval charm, exudes a mystic aura.

As I walk down one of its lanes, a local woman calling herself Bobby stops me to say I have a "lovely smile". Though I know it's a precursor to a sales pitch, I stop anyway; in part because a compliment makes me go weak at the knees, but more so because to speak to an Indian woman is a rare opportunity.

"I think Indian women are not talking to you, right?" she says. "This is because of our culture. They are worried others will gossip about them and think they are a loose woman. I am strange then, talking to you. But I believe Indian women should have more freedom.

"I work for an organisation that helps women in rural villages in Rajasthan. These women are in a terrible situation. They have no education, are married young, and have no money of their own. This makes them entirely reliant on their husbands. Even if their husband treats them very badly, they have no choice but to accept it.

"Our organisation encourages women like this to make craft products. We then sell the products here and give the money to the women. If they have their own money, they can be more independent."

I say, "If they have their own money, and they get treated poorly, then they'll be able to leave their husbands. Sounds good."

"Oh, no, they can't ever leave their husbands. We wouldn't recommend them to do that. Leaving your husband is a shameful thing to do."

Now the selling begins: She picks up a camel-knee massage ball and starts rubbing it up and down my back as she talks about the statues and trinkets spread over the stall. The ball on my back feels nice, but it's useless without a

woman to do the rubbing, and she's not selling any women —
not even a widow I could buy cheap and chuck after a few
uses.

I tell her I don't want the camel-knee massage ball or any
of the stuff; that even if all her wares were free, I wouldn't take
anything, as I don't need any of it. I'm not completely stone-
hearted, though, and give a ₹200 donation to her organisation. I'd like to think it will go to an abused woman in a rural
village, who will use it to break free from her tyrant of a
husband. Realistically, though, he'll beat her and take the
₹200 to upgrade his camel.

Plentiful around the fort are travel agents touting camel
tours. Tourists are suckers for camels, soon parted from their
cash when they see one of the lanky beasts. I'm a sucker; I
part with ₹1,800 for a "non-touristic" overnight safari, which
includes trekking and camping.

A French couple — Luca and Juliet — and I are driven
thirty minutes out into the wilderness, and dropped off with a
guide and his lackey. The guide says his name is Delsome-
thingindiansounding. He says no one ever remembers it, so to
call him Del Boy — a nickname bestowed on him years ago
by a tourist.

Five camels are coming for the trek. Del Boy says one of
them beat forty others in a race at a recent festival in
Jaisalmer. I tell him I don't want to ride that camel. I also don't
want the one called Bulldozer.

I ask, "Have you got any named Doris or Jonathan or
something like that?"

He offers one called Mr Kaluh.

That will do.

Del Boy shouts a command, and Mr Kaluh drops its front
knees to the ground, then a few seconds later its back knees.
This is the boarding position from which to straddle the blan-

ket-padded saddle. He shouts another command and — *whoosh* — the camel rises with me atop it. It's difficult to look dignified during this process. If a photo were snapped midway through, it would be debatable as to which face looked more ridiculous: mine or the camel's.

The camels walk in single file; each is roped to the one in front and behind. Del Boy walks ahead of the camel at the front, holding its front reign. As we go, they non-stop snort and belch and fart — only the camels, not Del Boy. The swaying, jarring gait of a camel is comparable to a bucking bronco set at a kid-friendly speed. Del Boy says he's never seen anyone fall off, but he would say that, in the same way Alton Towers prefer to promote how exciting a rollercoaster is instead of the risk of it going haywire and pulverising your limbs.

For a couple of hours, we traverse barren land that is apparently the Thar Desert but is more rocky than sandy. Wind turbines outnumber palm trees by a thousand to zero. It's certainly "non-touristic". The tourists are probably in the sand dunes, not out in the dirt. But at least there's absolute peace out here, and that alone is worth the cost. And there's wildlife to see too: groups of gazelles run by, eagles swoop from the sky, lizards dart between rocks.

I ask after a few hours: "How far have we come?"

"I don't know," says Del Boy. "I've never even seen a map of here. It's all in my head."

However far we've come, ₹1,800 is good value for all this time on a camel. I've now spent more time atop a camel than I have on a bicycle or at a car wheel — not many people can say that. And I've acquired flip-flop ninja badge no.76: camel trekking. These badges are earned by wearing flip-flops to do activities that flip-flops aren't classed as being appropriate for. Badges I'm yet to acquire include: no.42, cage fighting; no.84, running with bulls; no.749, high-wire walking.

When Juliet says she had a delicious chicken curry last night, Del Boy's eyes light up. "I love chicken," he says. "We can have chicken tonight if you want to buy one."

"There's a shop out here?" I ask, as I scan the bleak expanse.

"No," he says. "We just hope we see someone carrying a chicken, and try to buy it from them. If we offer ₹500, I think they'll sell us their chicken."

Crossing more wasteland hours later, we come across a heap of sand; Del Boy says it's a dune. It isn't. It looks like the Rajasthan Tourist Board gave a dozen blokes two-dozen buckets and told them to raid a golf course bunker.

Further on, through the heat haze rising from the baked earth, I see a man sat idly on a pile of dirt. One hut is nearby; probably he lives there. He hasn't got a television or a computer. He doesn't own any books — can't read anyway. His friends all live twenty-plus kilometres away. He has nothing to do but sit on a pile of dirt. A dog by the hut feebly barks and backs away from a herd of goats, failing to protect its territory against the scavengers. One of the goats has a threadbare piece of tinsel around its neck; perhaps its winner's garland from last year's pageant. It should be wary of the man sat on the pile of dirt: the devil finds work for idle hands.

After five hours of trekking, we come upon proper sand dunes — the real McCoy. (A golf course would have noticed if this much of their sand had been pilfered.) I sit high up on one and gaze over the windswept, rippling sand that bumps into the horizon. A lone black beetle plodding through the sand catches my eye. Wherever it's going, it's not getting there soon. I consider helping it along by chucking it as far as I can in the direction it's heading, but the last time I did something similar, people got angry. They didn't calm down even when I fetched back the hamster.

Del Boy and Rodders start a fire with twigs from a gnarled desert tree. From scratch, they cook curry and chapatis on top of a bent, burnt piece of metal which rests on stones over the flames. We sit in a circle around the fire to eat the fruits of their labour. They don't waste our limited water on washing up afterwards; instead, they use sand to clean the dishes. Amazingly, this works. I'll take a bag of sand on *Dragons' Den* and pitch it as an environmentally-friendly alternative to washing-up liquid. Half a million for a 5% share.

We set up camp by a bush for wind cover. No tents, just mats on the floor. The blankets Del Boy hands out are the same ones used for saddle padding. They reek of camel and sweaty crotch.

I fall asleep on a bed of sand beneath a duvet of stars to the sound of whispered words of French amour — "*Je t'aime ... Prends moi dans tes bras ... Embrasse-moi comme tu m'aimes ...*" — punctuated by camel farts.

UDAIPUR

Udaipur is known for its idyllic lakes and the ridged, wooded landscape surrounding their shores. While there are twelve lakes in total, it's the three located in the heart of the city that are the primary draw for visitors — both local and foreign.

Pichola is the most popular: Clustered around the fringes of its placid water are whitewashed *havelis* and ornately-turreted palaces. Rowing boats glide across it, bicycles leisurely circle it, and just-married couples pose beside it. A lot of just-married couples — this is India's wedding capital.

The iconic Lake Palace occupies an island in the middle of Pichola. It featured in the Bond film *Octopussy*. Dressed as a crocodile as lifelike as Barney the Dinosaur, 007 swam across to the palace looking for a Fabergé egg. Once there, Bond took a break from the mission to hide in some bushes to perv at women bathing in bikinis. It being India, I doubt he was alone in the bushes. Out of shot would have been a dozen guys in there with him.

The old quarter of Udaipur unfolds behind Pichola; its crooked, colourful lanes are full of twists and turns and charming niches. The further back you go, the more

Udaipur's extravagances evaporate into the realities of India, yet it's certainly laid-back by Indian standards.

Having exhausted my repertoire of photobombing gurns, spoiling several albums worth of once-in-a-lifetime shots in the process, my day takes a more productive turn: expanding my culinary skills at a cooking class. (Those skills currently max out at an omelette.) The class is at the home of a middle-aged woman — Shashi — who wears a blue-patterned sari that reminds me of a pair of curtains I had in my bedroom circa 1988.

She says, "I from small Rajasthani village. I marry man from Udaipur when I nineteen. Fifteen year ago, husband die. Brahmin wife not marry again after husband dead. My parents and husband parents also dead, so no money we have. Brahmin highest caste, so only some job can do: bank, teacher, doctor, for example. I no education at my village, so I not do this jobs. For years, I do secret work washing laundry.

"Then, five years ago, some tourist spoke my son and say they want learn Indian cooking. My son tell them I am good cook and bring them my house for teaching. That time, I speak no English. I very, very nervous. After that time, more and more tourist come. Now, this is my business, and I proud woman again."

A couple of Germans and a Chilean are taking the class with me. We'll make pakora, chutney, naan, chapati, paratha, and three curries. All the curries will be vegetarian. Shashi says she's never tried eggs or meat before. I ask, "Not even a hard-boiled egg for breakfast as a treat on your birthday?"

"No, never," she insists.

The five of us are jointly making the dishes, which means I can disguise my cooking ineptitude and not have to present shambolic work to the class. It took me fifteen shame-filled years, and thousands of pounds of therapy, to get over my spaghetti bolognese disaster at school. Shashi gets us mixing, mushing, pinching, pounding, chopping, peeling, slicing. It's too much, too fast for me; running before I can walk, algebra when I can't count past ten. I decide it's best to minimise my involvement, as we have to eat this after we cook it, and I don't want to eat rank food. So I buzz around waving a spatula, looking busy but doing little.

After taking a break to eat the pakora and chutney, Shashi reveals how to make what she calls her "magic sauce". She says that with chilli powder, coriander powder, turmeric powder, cumin seeds, anise seeds, oregano seeds, and garam masala, you can get the perfect taste for nearly any Indian dish. I note down the recipe but feel it's as much use to me as a porn mag is to a blind man.

Shashi eventually sees through my buzzing around with a spatula aloft trick. She takes it from me and makes me roll dough into shapes. This is harder than it sounds, even though she only wants me to make circles and triangles, not dodeca-hedrons. Whether trying to make a triangle or a circle, the result is something between the two — a tricle. Having a batch of tricles laid before me has uncovered me as a cooking fraud. "Very good", she says, then rolls up my tricles into balls and re-rolls them herself.

By the end of the class, I'm no nearer to being Gordonash Ramshi than I was when I started. My dream of starting an Indian restaurant is dead in the curry after I've dipped my toe in. I'll have to open an omelette restaurant instead.

In the afternoon, I visit a youth centre — part of a non-profit organisation set up by thirty-three-year-old Samvit, the bearded bandana-wearer who's family owns the homestay I'm sleeping at in Udaipur. He uses money generated from the homestay and other businesses to fund this centre and another one nearby. This one is a one-room stone building within a village in the hills set back from the lakes. Day-to-day, it's run by nineteen-year-old, bouffant-haired Bhopal. About thirty kids here today, but, says Bhopal, sometimes there are as many as fifty. It's open to all children in the area, and they don't need to be invited or to pay anything.

Bhopal says, "What we need are some walls inside to make the one large room into four smaller ones, so the children reading or studying aren't disturbed by those doing louder activities. And we also need a toilet. And a tap. One day, we hope computers too. Now we have one, but it won't switch on."

The daily timetable is handwritten on a piece of paper stuck to a pillar in the centre of the room:

> *3:00 - 3:10 - Cleaning the centre.*
> *3:10 - 3:20 - Hand and face washing.*
> *3:20 - 3:35 - Tooth brushing.*
> *3:35 - 5:15 - Choose your area: activities, workshop,*
> *   library or homework.*
> *5:15 - 5:40 - Meditation / yoga / prayer.*
> *5:40 - 5:45 - Hand wash.*
> *5:45 - 5:50 - Cookies / toffee.*
> *5:50 - 5:55 - Mouth wash.*
> *5:55 - 6:00 - Prayer -> Oh God*

Samvit says, "At first, we tried to teach them English and maths, but this was too difficult to do because of the lack of books and the range of ages. So now we focus on helping them with their existing schoolwork. Many don't have a quiet space at home to work or a family who have had an education to help them with it. And we offer them enjoyable educational activities too. So long as they're learning in some way, that's the most important thing."

Every extra hour spent learning matters even more than normal to kids like these, who's formal education will likely be short-lived. While 90% of children in India start school, less than a quarter go on to reach high school. That's three-quarters being sent out into the world half-baked; the latest generation of unskilled workers destined to languish in jobs that are low-paying and non-contractual. The competition for even those jobs is fierce, with India facing a formidable youth bulge. Every month, a million Indians turn eighteen years old. The fresh meat entering the workforce isn't offset by older Indians leaving it because the Indian demographic is heavily weighted towards the young: more than half its population are younger than twenty-five, and two-thirds younger than thirty-five.

Foreigners, a few of which are here today, come to help out at the centre — some for the day, and others for months. Samvit asks us to stand in front of the seated kids and give them a piece of advice. "Teach them something about life," he says. "Talk in short sentences and Bhopal will translate after each one."

"You go first," Bhopal says to me.

I slowly shuffle forward, buying myself as much time as I can to think up something profound and meaningful.

"Hello, I'm Mark. I'm from England. Erm, well, do you, err, like cricket?"

They nod their heads; a few yeses are uttered.

"Who's your favourite cricket player?" I ask a few of the kids.

I think: *Cricket? Why the hell am I talking about cricket? Cricket almost certainly has nothing to do with the meaning of life. It's barely even a proper sport.*

"Well, erm," I say next, "you know your favourite cricket player, err, well ..."

There it is again, the bloody c-word. I must get back on track. Come on, Mark, think: Go deep, blow their little minds.

"... if you want to be like them, you must work hard and never give up. Oh, and brush your teeth."

It's not a speech that's going to be quoted — outside the world of cricket, at least — but I manage not to swear or make any cock jokes, so it'll do.

As I listen to the other foreigners have a go, and I have more time to mull it over, I get some good ideas. I could have said: "A good attitude always improves a bad situation." Or: "Put yourself in situations you fear, and confront those fears." Or: "Life is like a box of chocolates: You never know what you're going to get."

(I've plagiarised the last of those, but I could have claimed credit for it. These kids won't have seen *Forrest Gump*. They haven't got a Netflix subscription between them.)

The life lessons from the other foreigners are as lame as mine. The kids must think Western education is a shambles if that's all we can serve up. "You racked up £10,000 of debt going to university, and you tell us to brush our teeth? You fucking dumbass." — That's what they would say if they knew enough English to say it.

For a couple of hours, the children study and play as they want. I'm not good with kids in freestyle situations, but I rummage around my mind for a game: *A game of cricket, maybe?* No, come on, stop with the bloody cricket. *Fetch?* No, that's demeaning — and I haven't got thirty sticks. I opt for an arm-wrestling competition. I try to make it as educational as possible by teaching them taunts in English: "... A quadriplegic could beat you ..."

Back at the homestay in the evening, Samvit and I engage in philosophical discussion while we eat tutti frutti ice cream. He tells me he's nearly enlightened. I ask how nearly.

He says 90%. I'm nearer to 9%, but I don't let that hold me back.

He asks, "Can you remember your first cup of chai? When was it? Where was it?"

I shrug and shake my head.

He continues: "Nobody can. Time doesn't exist. I'm thirty-three years old, but only a tiny amount of that time can I recall. Even *that* time I can't be sure about. I can't be certain what really happened, and what is only in my mind."

He also says, "When anything beyond the present moment no longer matters, and you stop asking how and why, there's no stress and no pressure. This is how to be happy. Though, of course, to be always happy is a myth. Happiness can't exist without unhappiness. Unhappiness is needed as a reference point, as a contrast to know when you're happy."

He talks a lot of sense. I find myself agreeing with much of what he says. And I definitely agree with his choice of tutti frutti ice cream — it tastes delightful. I wonder if you still enjoy tutti frutti ice cream when you're 90% enlightened or if it becomes a superficial pleasure beneath your higher state of mind. It feels too flippant to ask a wise man if he enjoys eating tutti frutti ice cream.

"The universe is infinite," he says, "yet all we know of it is what we see, hear, and touch. We each know so little; not even what's under this plate." He points at one on the table.

"There could be another dimension under it," I say.

"Yes, there may be. Anything is possible."

I pick up the plate. Under the plate is the table. I ask, "Could another dimension look like a table?"

"It may look different for everyone."

"So is this just a table? Or is it another dimension?"

"Who am I to say what it is? I've read a lot of books, talked to many clever people, but how can I know what is true and what is not? I can think this or think that, can give my opinions, but I can say nothing for sure."

Later, we add each other on Facebook. For a person who's 90% enlightened, he spends a lot of time liking photos of women. If he still likes women, he probably still enjoys tutti frutti ice cream too.

MUMBAI

Mumbai's most iconic landmark is the Gateway of India; it's a honey-coloured, decoratively-motifed Arc-de-Triomphe-lookalike that overlooks the Arabian Sea, built to celebrate the visit of King George V in 1911. The British were celebrating then; in 1948, it was the Indians when the last British troops to leave India passed through the Gateway, signalling the end of British rule. Sailboats and catamarans and tourist ferries circuit the calm waters around the Gateway; anchored further out are warships, cruise liners, cargo ships. This deep-water harbour handles more than half the country's maritime trade and is the reason for Mumbai's meteoric rise from fishing village to pulsating metropolis — the country's richest and most populous city.

The Taj Mahal Palace — India's premier five-star hotel — sits opposite the Gateway. A room costs ₹15,000 a night. Royalty and luminaries stay there. I'm not; nor will I be until I outsell Theroux. I instead book into a ₹750-a-night traveller ghetto down the road, where tales of India gripes leak through the flimsy wooden walls of the narrow brown rooms. Such an establishment lacks certain luxuries that paying an extra ₹14,250 to stay at the Taj gets you. A laundry service, for example — something I need. I can't put up with the camel stench on my jeans any longer. Essence of camel isn't a smell included in any high-end fragrances for a reason. I engineer an in-room DIY solution, a washing machine of sorts: shampoo and water poured into a plastic bag in a waste bin. After I clean my jeans, I wear them out wet; in the warm weather, they'll dry soon enough. The logic is right but the drying is patchy, meaning I walk around like a man who's pissed himself and either doesn't know or doesn't care.

On the vibrant main drag of Colaba — Mumbai's unofficial tourist district — zealous salesmen at street stalls sell knock-offs and bootlegs at throwaway prices in front of brand name shops selling authentic versions at full price. Some are more discreet with their pitches: A shady bloke sidles up as I stand looking through a bakery window. "Looking for something?" he asks. "Something *special*?"

"Some carrot cake, maybe."

He cuts to the chase: "Heroin?"

"No, a bit early for that. I normally only do heroin after I've had lunch. Sort of affects my appetite otherwise."

Not happy with the quality of carrot cake on offer, I go to Leopold Cafe — a famed Mumbai traveller haunt. Sometimes people dining here get scouted for extras roles in the Bollywood movies filmed at studios on the city's outskirts, so I spend an hour posing over my meal — I eat the eggs like Depp, the chips like De Niro. Surely they need a Spanish ninja in at least one of the nine hundred all-singing, all-dancing movies they churn out each year?

But I don't get that role — or any role. My acting was sublime, so I put it down to the pissy-looking patches on my jeans.

Back outside, waiting to cross the road, a man standing on

the opposite side, laden with an assortment of drums, sees this as a sales opportunity not to be missed, and a shouted exchange ensues:

"Brother, you want to buy a drum?"

"No, thanks."

"Yes, I think you need a drum. You want a big drum or a small drum?"

"No drum."

"Why don't you want a drum?"

"I don't need one. And I've got no space in my bag."

"So a very small drum is good for you. I have here, look." He takes a little drum from his back and holds it up to show me. "It's a very small drum, right?"

"Yes, it's very small. I don't want it, though."

"Brother, you take a long time to choose your drum."

"I'm not choosing a drum. I don't want one."

The crossing lights turn green, and we walk towards each other. He blocks my path in the middle of the road. "Brother, here is your drum," he says, trying to hand me the little drum. Ignoring him, I walk on. On reaching the other side and hearing ferocious horn-honking behind me, I turn and see the man still stood in the middle of the road, facing my way: "Brother, your drum."

Around the city, though, hands holding smartphones outnumber hands hawking trinkets or begging for rupees. Particularly so in Fort — the downtown business district, home to the Bombay Stock Exchange and the Reserve Bank of India, where sharply-dressed locals are out lunching: eating Subways and drinking Starbucks.

Other office workers prefer a home-cooked lunch and need not go home to get it. *Dabbawalas* (meaning "one who carries a box") on bicycles zip by with wooden crates of cylindrical containers packed with warm meals. The meals are collected from workers' homes in the suburbs in the late-morning, then delivered via sorting points and commuter trains to their city centre workplace in time for their lunch break. A crew of 5,000 implement this 125-year-old service to a daily customer base of 200,000. Mostly illiterate, the *dabbawalas* rely on a complex system of colours, numbers, markings, and abbreviations to ensure each lunch box makes it from the right kitchen to the right belly. They average only one mistake per 6,000,000 deliveries.

FedEx and Amazon were impressed enough with the speed and reliability of the *dabbawalas* to send executives to Mumbai to learn the secrets of their service. The proposal they presented at the board meeting on their return: thickos on bicycles drawing squiggles on boxes. Bicycles are much cheaper than drones, and otherwise unemployable syndromes can be paid £1 an hour to do the grunt work; don't be shocked then if you open your door one day soon to a drooling man with his trousers pulled too high clutching a package crayoned with hieroglyphics. A very special delivery.

Across Mumbai — and especially in Fort — are myriad stately buildings of architectural magnificence; stalwarts of old Bombay stood splendid in new Mumbai. The most extravagant of the bunch of beauties is the Chhatrapati Shivaji Terminus (formerly Victoria Terminus) — a gothic-esque structure of stained glass and turrets and spires and domes. As well as serving up an aesthetic treat, the UNESCO World Heritage Site also provides a practical purpose as one of India's busiest railway stations — up to 3,000,000 passengers daily. The history books say the British built Chhatrapati Shivaji Terminus, however, as with all of Mumbai's colonial-era buildings, that's not exactly correct. British hands may have drawn the designs but would have placed few bricks and beams. It would be more apt to say the British decided to build many grandiose buildings in Mumbai and then told the Indians, "No more samosas until you build them."

The spires of Chhatrapati Shivaji Terminus are visible from the nearby Oval Maidan, on which a half-dozen overlapping cricket games are in play. Some wear full-white regalia and sport expressions of extreme seriousness; others are playing for fun, wearing workwear and swinging for a six on every ball. No one has dared bring a football: In India, kicking a ball instead of throwing or batting it is considered as blasphemous as saying the elephant-headed Ganesha is nothing more than a glorified John Merrick. No cows on Oval Maidan or, indeed, anywhere in the city. Mumbaikars have evidently decided moos disrupting PowerPoint presentations and cowpat-coated foyers aren't consistent with the message that Mumbai is a modernised destination for business meetings. Autos, banned from downtown Mumbai, are also noticeable in their absence. Cars and taxis and buses are still bumper to bumper, but there's not the manic driving and horrific noise of other Indian cities. It's conclusive proof that auto drivers are to blame for the mayhem elsewhere.

A short walk from Oval Maidan is Marine Drive: a promenade cresting the curve of the Arabian Sea, lined with Art Deco apartment blocks — some of the most desirable addresses in the city. If you think it odd that Mumbai has any Art Deco buildings at all, you'll think it utterly bizarre that only Miami has more than Mumbai. The promenade is the preferred place for locals to escape the claustrophobia of central Mumbai; to stroll, ruminate, romance. Cosy couples cuddle on the stone wall by the sea, pestered by urchins selling roses; a man steps over them, clutching a kettle and a tower of paper cups, pouring chai as he goes. One guy stands teetering on the edge of the wall, seemingly about to jump into the water: I think perhaps a failing shampoo business has driven him to the abyss, but no, he steps down from the wall and fiddles with his flies — he was up there taking a piss.

Further along are three lads taking selfies, doing their best model poses: shades on and shirts undone and shoulders angled, looking into the distance. To look cool on Facebook isn't, I think, worth the cost of looking twatty in real life. The lads shouldn't be taking selfies here; so say not the narcissism police but the actual police. They've identified Marine Drive as one of sixteen places in Mumbai where taking selfies is dangerous, on the back of an eighteen-year-old girl recently falling in the sea mid-selfie and drowning. Selfie-related deaths are an increasing problem in the country; of the selfie deaths globally last year, half happened in India. Some walked backwards off gorges; others were taking a selfie with an oncoming train; a couple shot themselves in the head posing with revolvers.

At the end of Marine Drive is Chowpatty Beach; it's clean and quiet for a city beach — especially an Indian city one. Under the sun, smiley locals splash in the sea in front of blokes untangling fishing nets beside canoes. As I sit on the sand, dipping an ice ball into a cup of sweet-milk-and-mango sauce, I think that Mumbai is alright: a perfectly decent place to live. One day I'll come back for a long stay, maybe a month or three.

While Mumbai is one of the more liveable Indian cities, it is, however, still widely stained. Slums: An estimated 60% of Mumbaikars live in one, and the city is home to Dharavi, the largest slum in Asia. I've booked myself onto a walking tour of Dharavi. To pay for a tour of where poor people live is ethically dubious, I know. But I mount a two-pronged defence: 80% of the tour revenue is used for sports programs and education projects in the slum; and poor people are allowed to walk where my hotel is, so it's only fair I can walk where they live.

Dharavi lies on prime real estate in central Mumbai; it didn't at its beginning when it was marshlands on the northern fringe of the city, but over the course of a century, Mumbai has sprawled around it. Condominiums now surround the slum on all sides, each new one rising ever taller. The condo residents will have paid tens of millions of rupees for their slice of Mumbai. The average price of a home in the city is £150,000 — 50% higher than in Delhi.

Based on those prices, if I'm to have a stint in Mumbai, it may have to be in Dharavi, where monthly rents are as low as ₹500. If I were to stay in Dharavi, I wouldn't be lonely: It's not known exactly how many people live here, but seven-hundred thousand to one million is the estimate. In an area half the size of New York's Central Park, that makes it one of the most densely packed spaces on the planet.

Our group of eight — led by our guide Arish — cross a railway bridge and enter into the slum. The ground oozes and squelches in the beehive of unpaved passageways. Black foamy waste edges sluggishly along open drains running through metre-width alleys that are lined with homes on both sides. The lopsided, ramshackle homes come in a hodge-podge of styles, ranging from head-height shacks to multi-storey structures. Most look like something a child might draw: essential pieces — roofs and doors and windows — misplaced or missed out.

Draped cloth or propped plywood covers doorways, though the wonkiness of the ill-measured cuts means only partially, allowing glimpses of the cramped, confined innards and the crowded closeness of the dwellers, who can have no secrets from one another. Though most are one-room abodes, unpainted with a concrete floor, they look relatively homely.

On walls hang framed Gandhi portraits; on chairs lie neatly-folded clothes; on stoves cook pots of aromatic curries; in corners sit candlelit shrines. Some, however, are ultra-minimalist, lacking any furnishings at all.

None that I see have a toilet. There are communal ones but not enough. "Six hundred people share this one toilet block," says Arish. "Inside are three toilets for the men, three for the women."

As bad as they are, the dwellings here are no worse than those I've seen through bus windows when passing through innumerable provincial urban-armpits over the past weeks. Those living in Dharavi actually have it better than most slummers: they have access to water and electricity.

Living in Dharavi also means earning Mumbai wages, which are higher than elsewhere in the country. And the vast majority here are earning, for it's not a lounge for beggars. In addition to housing bus drivers, restaurant waiters, construction workers, and the like, some working white-collar jobs call it home too. Some residents can afford not to live here but choose to do so because of the low rent, the central location, and a network of family and friends. But for most they have no choice, are trapped here. Born in Dharavi, die in Dharavi: the all-too-common non-progression.

The slum is not only a place of residence but a workplace too. Beside the homes — and within some — are ten thousand workshops and small-scale factories: sewers and weavers, potters and printers and tanners, distillers and recyclers, and manufacturers of a thousand items. Clothes in your wardrobe labelled "Made in India" may well have been stitched here.

Of all the Dharavi micro-enterprises, recycling is the most prevalent, resulting in the slum being the city's de facto waste disposal unit. No rubbish collection day here; they have rubbish delivery day. That day is every day. What Mumbaikars discard tumbles down into Dharavi virtue of regiments of reverse-Santas: sacks slung over shoulders, they visit the city's homes, but instead of delivering desired goodies, they take away unwanted rubbish. Except it's not rubbish to the Santas and their Dharavi elves; to them, it's a free raw material to sort, recycle, repurpose.

Arish says, "Over 80% of the city's plastic waste finds its way to Dharavi, and more also comes from other cities."

Not just other cities, but other countries too: Outside one recycling workshop, she points at open sacks bursting with squashed yoghurt pots and says, "These are imported from the Middle East."

The thought of trash-layered India importing garbage makes the mind boggle.

Inside the sweltering workshop, bare-chested blokes engage in pungent drudge labour, engulfed in thick, black smoke. "After the plastic is sorted by colour and type," says Arish, "it's melted in workshops like this one and turned into pellets that can be reused."

At another workshop, she says, they make chairs from the recycled plastic. "They can't, unfortunately, export them to other countries because the method of recycling makes the plastic toxic," she adds.

Despite Dharavi keeping a million off the streets and producing over $700 million in revenue a year, the government wants to bulldoze the entire shantytown and redevelop the land. To them, it's a monument of backwardness, a stain on Mumbai's crotch. Crotch stains are fine when you're in kindergarten, hanging out with Bangladesh and Sri Lanka; not when you're trying to hobnob with Japan and America at a private members' club.

PALOLEM

I'm on the sleeper bus from Mumbai to Goa. A golden-orange-hued sun rises over a dense jumble of salad-bowl-green jungle. Banana and papaya and guava trees scatter the landscape. It's a different India again: Goan India.

We pass through Panaji, the capital of the state of Goa; it's something of an oddity for an Indian city: clean and green, quaint scenes. Low-rise, colour-washed houses with terra-cotta-tiled roofs, wooden-shuttered windows, and wrought-iron balconies line its streets; churches and cathedrals and basilicas border its squares; and signs above shops name the owners as being Fernandes or Mendes or Gomes.

These quirks are thanks to the Portuguese, who in the fifteenth century made landfall in Goa, starting the European colonisation of Asia. Priests came and evangelised, converting the locals — often by force — to Catholicism: "Comply or be burnt alive — up to you." Given that choice, I would also go to church and let people call me Gomes.

The Portuguese finally departed in 1961, 450 years after arriving. That was time enough for the invaders' influence to become entrenched, and the Goan vibe remains steadfastly

European, a piece of Portugal tacked onto the shore of the Arabian Sea.

I get off the bus 70 km down the coast from Panaji at Palolem — eighteen hours after leaving Mumbai. At Palolem, towering palms fringe a crescent-shaped, white beach that's bookended by rocky headlands — a beach that TripAdvisor recently ranked the second best in India and eighth best in Asia. Idyllic and tranquil, it's a fistful of cherries in the shit-cake — which is starting to taste less like shit, more like cherries.

Along the beach are abodes on stilts: some are flash pads; others sheds with beds. ₹1,000 gets me a night in one of the latter — that's painted bright pink. At only ₹1,000 a night — less if booked for a week or more — you could spend several months a year here: eating fresh fish, drinking cold beer, trying to touch your toes. You'll say you can't; say you have to work, pay the mortgage, take over the world. But don't forget the parable of the fisherman and the businessman ...

A vacationing businessman was walking along a beach near a village and came upon a fisherman taking several large fish from his little boat. The businessman, impressed, asked the fisherman, "How long does it take you to catch so many fish?"

"Not long, mister. Just two hour."

"Why don't you stay out fishing, so you can catch even more?"

"I not need more. This ok for feed family and sell one or two at market."

"If you're only fishing a short time each day, what do you do for the rest of the day?"

"Wake up late, go out sea for getting fish, then home for play my children. Afternoon, I do sex with wife and take rest.

Night time, I go village for meet friend. Drinking, sing song, dance."

The businessman, thinking the fisherman to be an uneducated simpleton, decides to offer him some advice: "You're not reaching your potential. You should spend more time at sea — at least eight hours per day — to catch as many fish as possible. Save the extra money you earn from doing this and use it to buy a bigger boat and to hire people to help you catch even more fish. Work hard like this for twenty years, buying more boats and hiring more people as you go. When you've saved enough, move to the city and set up a company to buy fish from villages all along the coast and export those fish to other countries."

"Sound like much work. Why I should?"

"You'll be able to retire when you're sixty and go to live by the sea. Every day, you can wake up when you want. You'll be able to fish, play with your kids, spend time with your wife, take naps in the afternoon, drink with friends every night."

"But mister, I already doing that."

The lesson: Don't wait until you're old to live the life you can live today.

There are fishermen at Palolem; their lean bodies beaching their catamaran-canoes. A decade ago, mostly only fishermen were here; yet despite word of Palolem spreading, it remains blissful and beautiful. Unlike some of Goa's other beaches: up the coast — at Vagator, Anjuna, Baga — Russians drunk on knock-off vodka and high on cheap opium stay up for days at a time and punch anyone who smiles at them.

Here, bums and tums are on show, and rums are in hand, as people lounge and listen to the waves and the birds and Jack Johnson's *Sitting, Waiting, Wishing*. The female flesh on show is all foreign; there's not a single Indian woman in a bikini — or even a granny-style bathing suit — but a few saucy tarts have their knees on display. I have my knees covered — the only option for a man who doesn't pack shorts — but have my shirt off. The sharp tan line around my neck makes me self-conscious: I look like I've had a face transplant from someone of another race.

An Indian woman — one the prettiest I've seen in India — speaks to me at one point. She says she's here with her mother, and points to a woman nearby. I smile at her mother; she smiles back. The girl and I chat for thirty minutes about nothing particularly interesting, but it's free-flowing, friendly, flirty. Being starved of female attention may be a factor, but I decide that if her mother offers her as a wife, I'll say yes — and not even ask for a PS4 as part of the deal. Then she puts a spanner in the works: she says she's a big fan of *Harry Potter*. If, like me, you're over thirty, anyone who's read *Harry Potter* is too young for you. If they're currently reading the books, you should be jailed for having talked to them. Not that you would get locked up for that in India, where there's a more laissez-faire approach to paedos — it's worse than the BBC was in the seventies. A third of the world's child brides are in India. Even the BBC drew the line at that.

At one of the beachfront restaurants, I browse the menu and place my order: "Fruit muesli, please."

"Sorry, fruit no, muesli no."

"Ok, I'll have porridge."

"Sorry, porridge no. Now end of season. Not much left. April 10, all beach huts close."

"What on the menu is still left?"

"Toast."

"And what else?"

"Just toast."

While eating my toast, a hawker — even paradise isn't perfect — approaches and tries to sell me stuff: a sarong, an ankle bracelet, an elephant statue. Someone else tries to persuade me to have a back massage. They're wasting their time pitching to people in restaurants. Trying to sell toast to someone shopping for a sarong or having a back massage is equally pointless.

I watch backpackers trudge past hunting for ₹250-a-night rooms, weighed down by backpacks far too big. Several times in the past weeks, people have asked me where my bag is when I'm carrying it at the time. "That's all you've brought with you?!" When I told them my tips — not packing a towel or shorts, trainers or spare jeans — some bowed to the travel guru; others gave me a look of pity that said I'd crossed the hobo line.

I see a man caked in sand from head to toe, who's just woken from a beer-induced beach snooze, stagger past like a creature from *Doctor Who* — a scary sight, making dogs and kids scatter as he lurches towards them. Another man walks to the end of the beach with a golf club and bag of balls and puts down a piece of wood topped with astroturf. It's cheaper than a golfing holiday, but he's sure to be pissed off: every shot will land in the sand or the water. Other balls in play are cricket ones, raining down like bombs on diners sitting at tables on the sand. The restaurant staff don't mind: half of them are the ones playing. The other half — between serving toast — crack on to single women, reeling off the mystical words that make foreigners "finding themselves" in India spread their legs.

Some tossers are jogging, an activity that should be banned on beaches as it makes everyone not jogging feel guilty about lazing around. Jason Bourne was doing that — jogging — on this beach (tosser!) at the start of *The Bourne Supremacy*. Palolem was his Indian hideout. Not a smart move: Loads of people staying here would have watched *The*

Bourne Identity and would have posted that they'd seen him: "Just seen Bourne at Palolem!!! He was eating toast while having a back massage! #Bourne #Palolem" No wonder the Russians found him.

Do you know where your hideout would be if you have to go on the run? It's worth thinking about as you never know when you might accidentally stab someone several times. I recommend Vietnam: It doesn't have extradition treaties with the UK or the US and is very liveable and inexpensive. Belarus and Madagascar are options on different continents. Or bluff your chasers — the Feds, the Russians, the Student Loans Company — and hide in the most obvious place: under your bed at home. Bourne should try that next time.

At night, lying in my pink shack, the only sound audible is waves breaking on the shore. This should be relaxing; however, every time I hear a loud one, I fret that it's the onset of a tsunami and leap out of bed to check if I need to flee. Experts advise getting at least thirty metres above sea level or three kilometres from the coastline. Don't take cover under a table — that's for earthquakes, not tsunamis. (Unless you have a *very* high-fucking-quality waterproof tablecloth.)

HAMPI

Where Hampi sits, once stood Vijayanagara — the capital of a Hindu empire that ruled southern India for two centuries. With half a million inhabitants, it was one of the world's largest cities; also one of its richest. Bejewelled with exquisitely expensive temples and palaces, it was described in its heyday as somewhere "that eye has not seen, nor ear heard, of any place resembling it upon earth". Then, in 1565, the empire suffered a catastrophic defeat at the hands of an alliance of neighbouring kingdoms. The victorious armies left little of Vijayanagara standing and massacred the hundred thousand residents who hadn't fled.

What before was a majestic metropolis now has the not-so-grand status of a village — a nondescript one at that. Tat is now touted where diamonds were once dealt. But people don't come to Hampi to visit the village; they come for the thousands of ruined buildings and monuments spread across a bouldered landscape of open plains and craggy hills. The ruins can be roamed, but a sign warns: "Do not go interior places lonely. There is possibility of getting attacked by robbers, thieves, and rapists. And no eatables or beverages given by unknown persons should be consumed." I'm more concerned about monkeys than rapists giving out cans of Coke: tribes of them charge about shrieking and attacking each other like the reincarnated spirits of slain Vijayanagara warriors.

Though there are many ruins, spread far and wide, there's little of the glory days left to see. The ruins are more like ruins of ruins, look like a three-year-old's first go at Lego. At only a handful can any shades of the grandeur of yore be sensed. The boulders are of more interest: there are tens of thousands of gargantuan proportions strewn all over like it once upon a time rained boulders. Some are in colossal hill-sized piles; others are stacked in inexplicable formations. It's beyond the work of man.

Scientists say the boulders are a natural phenomenon — something to do with erosion or the weather or whatever — but I've little faith in them and their test tubes. First they told me my great-great grandfather was a chimpanzee; then they started cloning sheep. I thought: What's the point in cloning sheep? They all look the same anyway. So screw the scientists; I'll side with the Hindus on Hampi: It's the fabled monkey kingdom of Kishkinda that's referenced in the *Ramayana* (an ancient Hindu poem). It describes a battle between a couple of warring monkey monarchs who threw boulders at each other.

Beside one boulder formation are hundreds of little piles of rock and slate, a dozen pieces in each; around them, a carpet of coconut husks and a dozen trees tied with bits of cloth. As I pass this scene from the occult, a bloke with only a few teeth greets me like an old friend. Mid-sentence, he abruptly pauses and says, "That there, on the inside of your hand; it's dirt or a mole?"

"It's a mole," I say. "It's always been there."

"You know what this means? To have a mole there on your hand? So that when you close it to make a fist, the mole is inside the fist?"

"No."

"It means you'll always have money coming into your hands. This is very, very lucky for you."

"But I also have a mole on the back of my hand, and it's larger than the other one. It means money will come, but money will go?"

He looks at me like I'm an idiot. "Don't be stupid." he says. "It's just a mole on the back of your hand. Why would that mean you'll lose money?"

Back in the village, I go to a cafe called Ravi Rose. I've been tipped off that they secretly whip up a potent concoction known as *bhang lassi* — a yoghurt beverage laced with *bhang* (a form of cannabis). As its use in India dates back thousands of years, I'm consuming it for cultural reasons, not for the sake of getting high — that's just a bonus. ₹400 gets me a large glass of the loopy juice. I gulp it down, then pay a fella with a motorcycle — Vijay — to take me to a lake a twenty-minute drive away. He says he'll come back to pick me up in four hours.

After thirty minutes of walking around the large but crap lake, I'm yet to feel any effects from the *bhang lassi*. I conclude I've been conned, that the *bhang lassi* was all *lassi*, no *bhang*. I leave the lake and follow lanes through fields of wheat and corn. After a couple of kilometres, I come upon a place called Whispering Rocks — a run-down backpacker haunt devoid of backpackers. But a half-dozen locals are here, larking about in the corner. I order food and a drink, and take a seat. Soon after, a psychotropic fogginess engulfs me: I know this because one of the Indians has come over and sat at my table, and he has three eyes — and I don't mean a red dot in the centre of his forehead.

"You know Dewsbury?" he asks me.

But that's not what I hear. "Does a berry what?" I say.

"Dewsbury."

"Uh? Jew berries?"

"Dewsbury near Leeds."

"Jews buried near Leeds? No, I don't know any."

"No, Dewsbury. It's a town near Leeds."

"Oh, Dewsbury. Err, yeah, right. What about it?"

"I'm Dewsbury."

"You're from Dewsbury?"

"No."

I rub my face with the palm of my hand.

He assaults me with blabber, lobbing phrase grenades at my mangled mind. Every other sentence is one he's picked up, accent and all, from foreigners who've passed through. He'll say one random thing in a Scouse accent, then the next in a Geordie one, with scant regard for typical conversation protocol of a sentence being even slightly related to the last one.

Fifteen brain-battering minutes later, the peanut butter on toast that I ordered comes. As soon as I take a bite, it registers as a mistake. It saps moisture from my already dry mouth and tastes like peanut-flavoured cardboard.

My state worsens. I'm Sketchy McSketch. I can barely speak, and I've got the twitches, and I think they're all talking about me. They probably *are* all talking about me — the nervous twitcher bumbling in the corner.

I decide I have to bail: abort, abort, abort.

I cut off Three Eyes while he's talking about Dewsbury again. I think he has a girlfriend there, or his uncle visited there, maybe, but I don't care if he's the damn Mayor of Dewsbury. I've had enough: "Erm, err, I've got to, err, go."

"But your peanut butter toast."

"Yeah, no. It, err, I mean, I'm, yeah, going."

"Now?"

"Right, yeah, bye."

If they weren't all talking about me before, they definitely are now; at the wacko who turned up, uttered more noises than words, ordered peanut butter toast, then bolted after eating one bite of it.

I make slow progress getting back to the lake; the lanes are like conveyor belts pulling me backwards. As I walk, to focus my mind and stop it spinning down insane thought trails, I listen to an audiobook on my iPod Touch. Richard Dawkins's *The Selfish Gene* is the wrong choice. I freak out when Dawkins says humans are robots for the genes contained within them, that our genes control all that we do.

I make it back to the pick-up point two hours early and sit on a wall, hoping to quietly pass the time and not have to deal with anyone. This plan is scuppered by a bloke sat on a rock beside a boat. He's straight over to me and says something I don't catch, even though he repeats it three times. He dips his hand into his *lungi* and pulls out some little something-or-others, which he presents in the palm of his hand. They look like little stones; the same little stones that are all over the ground.

I say, "Err, no, erm, thank you. I don't need any, err, little stones."

Then a new guy shows up, shuffling down a slanted stone slab to the left. He comes to a stop, then squats and lifts his *lungi*. I see the chute opening, the torpedo launched.

The stone merchant is suspicious of the newcomer; he puts his goods back in his *lungi*, gets in his boat, and rows off.

With them both gone, I question if either were ever here, if they were only figments of my robotic mind. Then I start doubting everything — even if the boulders really exist. I do what probably no one in Hampi has ever done before: walk around tapping boulders to check they're real.

As my mind continues to unravel, I start fretting that I'll be the subject of one of those "Please help, my child is missing in <insert foreign country>" posts that spread on Facebook. A concerned mother makes such a post after not hearing from her child for a week. She fears her child has been kidnapped and sold into the sex trade. Then they turn up naked in a cave, convinced they're an aardvark, having gotten too high.

When a group of Indian couples pull up on three motorcycles and get their phones out to take photos by the lake, I see it as an opportunity to fast-track my way out of here. Not by stealing one of their motorcycles — a drunk move, not a stoned one — but by using one of their phones to call Vijay to ask him to pick me up early.

I stammer my request, and one of the girls hands me her phone. I'd have preferred her to take the paper with his number on and call him for me; if you have to ask why, I bet you've never been unduly stoned in front of norms. Knowing that failing to carry out what should be a simple task will out you as a stupefied space cadet, 2 x 2 becomes 143 x 37.

I look at the paper, then the phone, then the paper again. I start pressing numbers: eight-seven-six. It's a good start; three out of three. But then both the paper and the phone go blurry, and I lose track of which numbers I've entered and which I haven't. I take a deep breath and tell myself, *Come on, you're a robot, you can do this. R2-D2 wouldn't blow a fuse dialling up C-3PO.*

The sound of a cough makes me look up. They're all staring at me. Specifically, staring at the phone in my hand on which I appear to have declared a unilateral thumb war. I've no idea how long I've been trying to enter this phone number. It could be seconds, it could be minutes. The sun hasn't set, so at least it hasn't been hours. But however long it's been, it's evidently been too long.

I check where I'm up to: eight-seven-six-two-two-three-two-two-three. That's not right: too many twos, too many threes. I must have been pressing twos and threes when thinking about R2-D2 and C-3PO.

"Do you want me to do it?" the girl asks.

"Yeah," I say, hanging my head in shame, outed as a doped-up dunderhead.

MADIKERI

I took a daytime bus from Hampi to Maderiki; my first in a while, after a series of overnight sleeper buses took me from Jaisalmer to Hampi. I slept well on those night buses; I had a bed to myself and, on the aisle side, a plastic partition and a curtain to block out other passengers. (I could have watched sexy kiss videos with my busmates being none the wiser.)

While those journeys were comfortable(ish), travelling through the night meant missing out on scenery along the way. I'm pleased I didn't miss the scenes from Hampi to Maderiki; it was India at its best, rural and unspoilt. The land was fertile, a hundred shades of green; full of rice and wheat fields, banana plantations, coconut palms. Life in the remote communities stripped of modernity was serene and slow, and the villagers seemed happier than their northern counter-parts. I doubt they have more rupees to their name, but the bountiful landscape and bluer sky made them seem more well off.

Today, I follow a path through a mist-drenched plantation; coffee plants cascade beneath a canopy of oak trees wrapped in pepper vines. It's one of many coffee plantations in Coorg, a hilly region that's part of the Western Ghats (a chain of mountains that stretch 1,600 km along the west coast; home to more than 30% of all plant and animal species in the country).

You're thinking: *Coffee in India? I thought they all drank tea?!*

While it's true that India is a nation of tea drinkers, some love a cheeky coffee or two as well. And "some" in a country of more than a billion equates to rather a lot. The "some" are on the rise too: the coffee market has doubled over the past five years, mainly due to a burgeoning middle class in urban areas, who will pay ₹150 to sit with a coffee in air-conditioned comfort to avoid standing with a tea in the sweaty street — even though the latter is ₹140 cheaper.

But despite the rapid increase in coffee consumption, tea won't be toppled as king of the drinks any time soon. Per capita, India's tea consumption per year is 176 cups; for coffee, it's 15 cups.

Not all of Coorg is so exotic. An almost British feel to some of the scenery. In this "Scotland of India" — as some call it — I amble down rocky lanes, past olde cottages, through verdant woodlands, over grassy pastures. The rainy season isn't for a few months, yet the land is flush with greens, peppered with wildflowers.

I come out of a field into someone's backyard. A woman is stood a few metres away, putting laundry on a line. She turns and looks at me, says nothing and expresses no emotion, then turns and carries on with the chore, unperturbed by the foreigner unexpectedly in her garden. An Indian showing up uninvited in a backyard in Scotland would receive a different response: he'd be sworn at and beaten with a rolling pin. In the US, he'd be shot in the leg — then the police would come and shoot him in the head.

I walk past the woman and through her gate onto a lane leading away from the house. On the lane, I pass a house with an elderly, infirm man laid on a wicker bed out front; he looks like he has weeks, not months, left. It's a common sight in India, where retirement homes are rare. For Indians, putting their parents in third-party care because they can't be bothered to look after them is seen as shameful. Most are keen to avoid the shame: a 2012 survey found three-quarters of Indian women over sixty live with their married children. In the West, people say they don't want to pack off their parents but make an excuse and do it anyway. Any children I have will certainly do it to me: their sweet revenge for sending them out to work when they turn eight years old to fund my early retirement.

On a road on the outskirts of Madikeri — Coorg's largest town — I pass a *lungi*-wearing bloke with a *tilaka*-spotted forehead stood in front of the bright-blue door of a whitewashed building. He motions me to come to him. As I near him, he goes indoors; he reappears with a piece of folded newspaper in which is a mix of dried coconut, apple, and corn. Beaming broadly, he offers it to me. It looks tasty; I take it and ask, "How much? ₹10? ₹20?"

He smiles and shakes his head. "No rupees."

Lining the road are signs that advertise homestays — side-businesses set up in the mid-nineties to counter fluctuating coffee prices. The one I'm staying at is part of a large estate, up in the middle of nowhere. It's run by Tim, a forty-something bloke wearing funky specs and chunky boots.

"Are they for eating?" I ask, pointing at a pigsty near my room.

He says, "These are pets for us, but other people shoot theirs then sell them at the market. A 100 kg pig is worth about ₹15,000."

If you think shooting a pig is barbaric, believe me, there are worse ways to do the job. In a village in northern Thailand, I saw a pig killed with a hammer. Six heavy thuds landed on the swine's head; each caused a blood-curdling squeal. I swore I'd never eat meat again. And I didn't — until the morning after when the dead pig was the only option for breakfast.

Tim gives me a tour of the grounds in his jeep, a berry-red Mahindra from the sixties. A sticker on the front says: "Do drink coffee and drive". We edge along a bumpy track carved into the slopes of the forest; ravines drop away to our side.

"We grow both Arabica and Robusta coffee beans," he says. "Robusta is the stronger and cheaper of the two but has less flavour. Though we can sell Arabica for a higher price, there's more risk with it as it's more prone to disease. The beans taste different to those grown in Colombia, Brazil, and Africa. Indian ones are better, more flavoursome."

It's standard for Indians to believe that the Indian version of something is the best version of it. I've had Indians tell me everything from cars to textiles to women are better in India than elsewhere. The rest of the world rarely agrees.

Indian coffee beans aren't as lauded as their Latin American and African cousins for historical reasons. From the forties to the nineties, all coffee growers in India had to sell their beans to the Indian government, who bulk sold them to the Soviet Union. The commies cared about cost not quality, so the coffee farmers weren't bothered if their brewed beans tasted like barf — they were paid the same if it did or not. But the reputation of Indian coffee is on the rise. The country is the sixth largest coffee producer in the world, and more than three-quarters of its crop is exported. Coffee snobs Italy are the biggest recipient. Nescafe and Nestle use Indian beans in their blends too, so if either of those supply your caffeine hit, what you sup may come in part from Coorg.

A note of elephant excrement is an indication that your

brew is Coorg-grown; splodges of it are splattered around Tim's estate. He says, "Wild elephants often come. We no longer bother with our rice paddies because they kept trampling and ruining the crop. We see the dung and the damage a lot more than we see them, which is good as you don't want to see one face to face: they're likely to charge at you."

They're more deadly than you think, killing more people globally per year than tigers or sharks do. Disney glossed over that in *Dumbo*.

Back at Tim's house, we sit under a fig tree on a veranda that overlooks the estate, sipping freshly brewed coffee. Crickets, beetles, moths, and other creepy crawlies swarm to the light that hangs from the tree.

"This estate has been with our family for over 150 years," Tim tells me, "since the time of my great-great-grandfather. The land passed down through the generations, each time to the eldest son. I studied business at university, then started a telecoms company, but I came back to take over the estate when my father could no longer run it."

I ask if he has children to pass it on to.

"I have two daughters; I'll give it to them when I'm too old to look after it. It's up to them what they do with it — if they want to keep it or sell it."

Such a scenario is increasingly happening in India, with the latest generation being forced to choose between tradition — in continuing the family business — and modernity — with a career in IT or marketing or engineering. Many choose the latter. In doing so, masses of young people are leaving rural areas for urban ones. By 2030, it's estimated that 40% of Indians will live in cities — up from 11% in 1900.

I wish my great-great-grandfather hadn't been such a lazy mofo so I'd have the choice between tradition and modernity. What a selfish sod he was, not passing down a coffee plantation or fruit orchard or ganja farm. I would have cashed it in — no doubt about it. In theory, it's days in the sun and money growing from the ground. But the reality is long hours, prayers to the weatherman, and living in fear of elephants.

Tim says, "My great-great-grandfather was the Deputy Commissioner of Coorg when the British were here. They appointed him to the position after he helped quell a rebellion. He was highly respected. He built Coorg's first girls' school at a time when most thought there was no need to educate girls."

He tells me about his great-great-grandfather shooting a tiger: "Even back then, when there were many more than there are now, it was a rare and difficult thing to do. He put the carcass on a bamboo pole and paraded it around the town. And there was a tradition that a man who killed one should be wedded to its soul in a special ceremony. A British officer was at the ceremony; he drew a sketch and wrote an account — both are in a museum in England."

As Tim bids me goodnight, he gives some parting advice: "Life isn't short, but minds are small. My great-great-grandfather died at only thirty-eight but accomplished so much. We can all do such a lot in the time we have."

Feeling inspired, I add a new item to my to-do list: see a tiger or elephant in the wild. I'll take a photo of it, then print it off and stick it on a bamboo pole, and walk about the streets, showing it off. Not as cool as parading the carcass of a tiger, but times have changed, and I don't want to be cyber-lynched — as I was before: I had to close my Twitter account after I posted a picture of me wearing a leopard-skin thong. The abuse I got was vile — and that thong wasn't even made from a real leopard.

WAYANAD

I'm in Tholpetty Wildlife Sanctuary being driven around in a jeep. Forest lines the sides of the track; flora and shrubs and creepers run wild. The driver is Hussein, a smiley, gangly guy in his twenties, who with an additional set of arms and legs would pass as the world's biggest and nicest spider.

Around 30% of the world's Asian elephant population, and 15% of all the wild tigers in the world, reside in these forests that are part of the Western Ghats. 15% sounds like a lot of tigers but it's 15% of a small number. The most recent tiger census — from January 2015 — showed there are now only about 2,200 tigers left in all of India. In the 1930s, there were 40,000.

Hussein says, "This year, I haven't seen any tigers. Last year, I saw one only six times."

Despite the roaming animals, some locals walk along the side of the track. Hussein says walking around in pairs is safe as a tiger won't attack if it's outnumbered, but I spot a flaw in this safety strategy: two tigers on a date. Four people in this area were killed by tigers last year; nine more people by elephants. I'd much rather be killed by a tiger than an elephant. At your funeral, if it's read out that a tiger savaged you, people will say, "Well, at least it was a cool way to go." If they hear an elephant stood on you, people — your Mum included — will laugh.

In the jeep with us are four blokes from France; there's a competition between us to see who can spot the most animals. I focus my efforts on elephants, reasoning that being the largest they'll be easier to see. Easier, but not easy, as the sanctuary covers a lot of ground. Seeing one is far from guaranteed. A few cases of mistaken identity early on. When you're actively looking for an elephant, everything suddenly looks like an elephant. Large rocks, cars in the distance, houses in the woods — none of which on an average day you'd mistake for an elephant — become so elephant-like that if you were asked on *Who Wants to Be a Millionaire?* ...

"Now, the final question, for a million pounds: *Is that an elephant?* Your choices are:

A: No

B: Could be

C: Probably not

D: Abso-fucking-lutely YES!!!"

... You'd say, "I'll play; it's D."

There aren't only elephants and tigers here. "There are often mongoose in this section," Hussein says at one point. I don't want to seem dense by asking him what a mongoose looks like. I think it might be a horse-like animal with antlers. For five minutes, that's what I look for; then I remember that's a moose. I spend the next five minutes looking for a goose with learning difficulties.

One of the French spots a posse of spotted deer frolicking in the fringes of the forest (five points to him). Further on, the faces of a couple of water buffalo peep through some grass. I see them but Hussein calls them out before I do (two points to him). Then Hussein spots a wild chicken — that's scraping the barrel but still earns him a point. Hussein redeems himself with a group of a dozen langur monkeys. It propels him well into the lead.

I haven't got any points yet, but if I'm still losing with only seconds left on the clock, I'll get out the jeep and kick over an anthill.

With only ten minutes of the safari left, a pile of fresh elephant dung in the road raises hopes. A few minutes after — nearly two hours since we set off — Hussein brakes and points over the road. "There! An elephant!"

He's right; it's an elephant — large rocks don't have big ears and a trunk.

I congratulate Hussein. He's still only getting one point for it, though. There's nothing in the rulebook saying an elephant is worth more than an ant.

We return to Varnam Homestay, where Hussein works and the Frenchies and I are staying, along with half a dozen other foreigners. It's a C-shaped, peach-coloured building bordered on three sides by a tropical garden. Hammocks crisscrossing between jackfruit trees sway gently in the breeze over a green lawn that leads to a games area with a badminton court and a ping-pong table. It's only a swimming pool short of being a resort.

The homestay is owned and run by Beena and Varghese, a kind-hearted, middle-aged couple. Varghese is a real character; he looks like Freddie Mercury and has the mannerisms of Borat.

"I'm both a farmer and a policeman," Varghese tells me.

I say, "Planting rice by day, catching criminals by night; like a rural Batman?"

"I don't have to catch any criminals," he says. "There's no crime in Wayanad."

When Paul — one of the guests — complains about sunburn, Beena concocts a herbal remedy to cure it: basil paste. She tells him to massage it into his skin, leave it for fifteen minutes, then wash it off; and then do the same again. Paul tries it and says it works, says his sunburn is much less sore.

"There's one problem, though," he adds, lifting his shirt, "it stains your skin green and won't scrub off."

So before you start slathering your-sunburnt-self in basil paste on your next holiday, first do a cost-benefit analysis: while the pain might be relieved, you'll have to spend the rest of the week walking around like an Incredible Hulk imper-sonator.

Beena says, "We always use natural remedies; they're the best ones." When I ask for some other examples, she says, "If a man is going bald, he should rub bison dung on his head. It will make his hair grow back."

"Surely that can't work?" I say.

When she insists that it does, I say, "Ok, I'll test it tonight; I'll rub some above my top lip before I go to bed, and let's see if in the morning I have a moustache."

"Oh, no, *that* won't work," she says. "Bison dung is only for growing head hair. To grow a moustache, a man should put sloth oil on his top lip."

"Sloth oil? What's that?"

"You kill a sloth and cut it open, then heat it until the juices come out."

Hussein takes the guests around the garden. He shows us trees and plants sprouting grapefruits, cardamom, cinnamon, avocados, tamarind, papayas, turmeric, mangoes, oranges, tapioca, ginger, limes, cacao, chilli, basil, mint ...

As he's showing us the eight types of banana growing in the garden, Megan — a doctor — mentions that potassium is a good choice for poisoning someone because it stays in the body only a short time after. I thank her for the tip but question its practicality. The problem is your victim will be suspicious you're up to something by the time you're forcibly stuffing the hundredth banana down their throat.

"And here are vanilla creepers," Hussein says. "Vanilla is the second-most expensive spice in the world. The most expensive is Saffron. It takes 1,500 handpicked flowers to get a single gram of saffron."

If someone had given me a bag of saffron for an Xmas gift, I'd have called them a tight-fisted twunt. I'll no longer do that; I'll give them a hug instead, and double-check they know when my birthday is.

Hussein next shows us cashew nuts — they grow on top of pieces of *fruit*. I didn't know that. Then he points out pineapples sprouting from the ground. I always thought they hung from trees — like coconuts. I question how much I know about the world, and if — despite long disputing the claim — I am indeed an imbecile.

In the evening, the guests sit at an outdoor table for dinner. On the table is a row of pots, each filled with home-cooked organic dishes made with ingredients from the garden. I lift the lid off one of the pots and see beef curry — juicy chunks swimming in a thick brown sauce. I think: *Is it a trap? Is Varghese waiting for me to tuck in, and then he'll spring from under the table and put handcuffs on me for the heinous crime of cow-scoffing?*

I look under the table; he's not hiding there. I ask Beena what the deal is.

She says, "We eat beef here in Kerala. It's one of only a few states in India that it isn't illegal."

This creates a dilemma: I love beef; it's the best of all the meats, and I've missed being able to eat it. But I've been 100%

vegetarian while in India — thinking it's less likely I'll get sick, and also because the veggie options are so tasty. It's been good being a vegetarian; I feel healthy and I've enjoyed looking down my nose at filthy carnivores. But I do like the look of this beef. I shouldn't, but I want to ... And I damn well will! I chew a chunk; it slips down my throat. *Oh, beef, how I've missed you.* I get a second portion; then a third. I'm binging on beef, I'm off the wagon — pass me the chicken too.

Today is Beena and Varghese's twenty-fifth wedding anniversary. As Varghese cuts the cake bought for the occasion, I ask him what's the secret to twenty-five years of marriage.

He says, "Beena, what's the secret to twenty-five years of marriage?"

"Patience," she says.

But I think the real answer is having your wife speak on your behalf.

Varghese tell us — in between licking cream off his fingers — "Our families arranged our marriage. Beena and I met just one time before our engagement party — for ten minutes only. After our engagement party, the next time we met was on our wedding day."

Like Beena and Varghese, the majority of Indians have their marriage arranged for them. Of the ten million weddings that happen a year in India, about 70% are arranged marriages, 25% are semi-arranged marriages, and 5% are unarranged marriages.

For an arranged marriage, parents — often with the help of their extended family — search for a mate for their child via their community, newspaper adverts, and matrimonial websites. They screen, research, and interview potential matches, with the caste of the candidate, their level of education, and their occupation some of the critical considerations.

Once the selection process is complete, the parents present the chosen one to their child. Refusing to accept who they've been assigned isn't a feasible option; it runs a high risk of being cast out of their own family for slighting their parents.

In a semi-arranged marriage — still mainly an urban phenomenon — the process is for the most part the same as for an arranged marriage; there's a key difference, though: parents allow their child to turn down the chosen one. Should they do so, the parents will make a new choice.

A son or daughter finding someone of their own accord is restricted to only the most liberal of Indian families. Even with such a family, a child having a merry-go-round of partners in their teens and twenties is a no-no. Tindu (Tinder for Hindus) is still a long way off.

To many Westerners, the concept of arranged or semi-arranged marriages is outrageous. But the Indian approach of looking at marriage like solving a maths equation, rather than writing a romantic novel, has a strong statistic to support it: only 1% of marriages end in divorce in India. In the West, divorce rates are over 30%.

Still, I wouldn't trust my Mum to choose a wife for me. You should see some of the clothes she's bought me as gifts. A couple of years ago, she bought me a pair of multi-coloured swim shorts that had a giant skull and crossbones on them.

I told her: "I can't wear them, Mum."

"Why not? They're nice."

"Yeah, for a prepubescent, colour-blind pirate."

FORT KOCHI

Fort Kochi is a town on the Malabar Coast — a bucolic, tropical slither of coastline in south-west India. It's a former trading post of exotic goods, which attracted Arab, Jewish, Chinese, and European traders as far back as the fourteenth century. The traders exported Indian spices and tea, and imported their religions and architecture. It now resembles a quaint village in Surrey. Elegant colonial-era houses, built by the pepper barons of the past, line its somnolent streets; their facades sunburnt and monsoon drenched, coated with manes of ivy. I'm starting to think that perhaps I was too quick to judge India: It might not be a shitcake with cherries in it, but a cherry cake with lumps of shit in it.

Kochi has a beach; it's packed with Indian families who sit on the sand and survey the Arabian Sea, where vessels as varied as canoes, ferries, trawlers, and warships pass by. Fully-clothed people wade into the water, and novelty kites twist and turn in the breeze, and bells ding-a-ling from wacky-coloured ice cream trucks. A porky baldie fishing stops me for a chat and says, "The Kerala environment very, very good. The best with the Alps. Oxygen in Kerala air 90.9089%. No,

998.9%. Wait, no, 9890.90%. No … Anyway, it's high oxygen percent. If you live Kerala, you will upgrade life five year more. Soon Kerala will sell our air. Chinese people will buy it in bottles so they can upgrade their life also."

I'm here with Aoise, a hippy-outfitted, blonde-haired woman. Locals keep asking us to pose for photos with them. As much as I'd like to think we're co-stars in these photo-shoots, I never normally get so many requests in a short spell. It's clear Aoise is the star attraction. She's Baby Spice; I'm Sporty.

Some of the guys ask me if they can take a one-on-one selfie with Aoise. She tells them, "Ask *me*, not him," and is annoyed that they're treating her like my property.

I tell them, "Yes, you can, but be careful with her. I'll be checking for scuffs and scratches when you give her back."

Aoise says to me, "Sometimes I want to say no because, really, what are they doing with these photos? I try not to think about it."

I've thought about it, and I'm sure dirty deeds are done with the photos.

Aoise tells me about a place called Auroville that she's been living at for the last five years. She says it's near Pondicherry on the eastern coast and is a sort of utopian society built in the sixties. The more she tells me, the more I think it sounds like a cult with a lot of sex. I make a note to visit. She later says that sometimes snakes find their way into her hut at Auroville. In the rainy season, she says, scorpions the size of cats too. I adjust my earlier note: *Visit Auroville (NOT in the rainy season)*.

Beside the beach is the Dutch Cemetery — the oldest European cemetery in the country — where wild growth over-runs blackened tombs, and a five-minute walk along the shore are the Chinese fishing nets — Kochi's most-snapped attraction. The fourteenth-century contraptions — introduced by Chinese immigrants — are made of roped together teakwood beams that angle into the sea like hovering alien arachnids. Men plunge the nets below the water using a stone-weighted pulley system, then smoke and gossip and pray to the sea gods before raising the nets again. The fishy hauls plucked from the water make their way to shacks behind the nets, where they're gutted and sold fresh for use in Kochi's famed curries. Around the shacks, lion-like cats laze, well-fed on scraps and well-exercised chasing rats away. Men laze too, under thick-trunked shady trees, turning benches into makeshift mattresses. On the streets set back from the fishing nets, shops sell fusty rugs, bronze deities, pashmina shawls, and manufactured handicrafts. Some specialise in DIY fragrances; outside those are glass bottles with their contents penned on sticky labels: rose, tea tree, jasmine, lavender, sandalwood ... In theory, a splendid idea; the unfortunate likelihood, though, is conjuring up something more like catnip than Chanel.

At the SVM Ayurveda Centre, I pay ₹1,200 for an hour-long massage, keen to rid myself of the many aches and pains inflicted during long days and longer nights on buses and trains. There's more to Ayurveda — one of the world's oldest holistic healing systems — than massages (like diet, exercise, and lifestyle) but I'm looking for a quick fix that I can do lying down. I'm hoping it hits the massage sweet spot: something between a tickle and a wrestle.

The masseuse is an egg-headed fella wearing a checked apron. He takes me to a small, unlit room; a fan whirs over a wooden treatment table. Through the open window mingle the bleats of goats, the tweets of birds, the laughter of children.

I ask him what the difference is between an Ayurvedic massage and other types of massage.

He says, "Special herbal oil is used for an Ayurvedic massage." He points at four glass bottles of amber-coloured oil on the window ledge. "Here we use a secret recipe of coconut oil with ten herbs."

Then he says, "Take your clothes off."

"Right, ok. Here?"

"Yes."

"And put on that towel on the table?"

"No. That's for showering with afterwards."

I wait a few seconds to see if he's going to leave. He doesn't, so I strip off naked in front of him. He holds up something: a piece of string with a few sheets of toilet paper hanging from it. He wraps the string around my waist and ties it at the back. Then he moves behind me, reaches down between my legs, gets the end of the tissue, lifts it up between my legs, and tucks it into the string above my crack.

He tells me to lay on my back on the table, then uncaps one of the bottles of oil and begins basting me like a turkey. He works like a sculptor, his fingers and thumbs moulding me into shape. After a while, he tells me to sit up cross-legged on the table. "Not that way," he says, grabbing my shoulder and spinning me around, like a pot on a wheel. Then he rubs oil into my hair and pushes it forwards and upwards into the style of a Korean pop star. While I look ludicrous, I smell lush — a cross between a Bounty and the Body Shop.

"Now lie on your front," he says.

I do so and he undoes the tissue from the back tuck and lets it lay between my legs. The oil has turned the tissue soggy and brown, making it look and feel as though I've shat myself. If anyone looks through the window, they'll think I'm an adult baby having my nappy changed.

He next massages my back and buttocks. My arse has never before been massaged — there are muscles I didn't know existed. For a split second, I panic he's about to slide a finger up the hole, but I think his hand just slipped on the oil.

While not the most pleasant experience, on the whole the Ayurvedic massage proves to be money well spent as my aches have abated. But I'll leave it a while before the next one; people will think I enjoy nude, oily, bottom massages if I have one too often.

After the massage, I go to a theatre to watch a Kathakali performance — advertised as "A dance-drama inspired by Indian folklore and mythology, which combines facets of opera and ballet and pantomime."

A hairy-chested, big-bellied bloke walks onto the wooden stage and sits on a stool, from where he croons while playing something resembling an accordion. A couple of similar-looking guys appear and stand to his left, rhythmically rapping drums with rolling finger movements. A pair of farci-cally grotesque performers then emerge onto the stage, outfitted in flamboyant, billowing costumes and elaborate, extravagant headwear that's larger than their actual heads. Thick, vivid makeup entirely covers their faces to appear as though a mask is worn, making them look almost clown-like. No dialogue in the performance; only hand gestures, facial expressions, rhythmic dancing. The attention to detail is insane with micro-movements of the eyebrows, eyeballs, cheeks, nose, and chin all minutely worked out and denoting a meaning. And each movement and gesture is precisely in time with the beats of the vocal and percussion accompa-niments.

Impressive as it is, the problem is that without words the storyline is something of a mystery. Little can be deduced from the deformed, disturbing characters. It's like watching

CBeebies on a comedown. I think it's a love story between a king and a transgender geisha. They're cosy, and all is well; then he suddenly loses his shit — possibly on realising she has a schlong — and slices her up with his sword.

In the evening, I return to Reds Residency, a boutique homestay with hotel comforts: air-con, hot water, good wifi, cable TV. It's the hosts that make a homestay, though, and Philip and Maryann — friends with Varghese and Beena from Wayanad — are as great a pair as their friends are.

A lad lives in-house to help them out. He's from up north, a long, long way from here, and I ask Philip why he hired someone from so far away when there must be plenty of people here he could have hired.

He says, "I learnt my lesson about that. The problem when you hire a local is that there's a never-ending list of sick and dead relatives they come up with to get the day off work. I once hired a local who was always doing that. I, at last, caught on and realised it was bullshit when the bugger had his fifth grandparent die."

Philip has several businesses. He says, "I'm setting up a new one for my son. He's just come back from studying engineering in the Ukraine. He loved it there; it took some getting used to, though. One time he put his jeans outside to dry, and it was so cold they froze solid. When he tried to break the ice off them, they snapped in two."

When I ask if he's thinking of retiring soon, he says, "Just one more year."

Maryann laughs. "He's always saying just one more year!" She adds, "But we won't retire from the homestay for a long time. We love being around people. We enjoy meeting guests from around the world and hearing about their lives and travels. The homestay doesn't feel like work to us."

Their enthusiasm touches me; it makes me think: Maybe

I'll start my own homestay. Instead of busing myself around the world, the world can come to me on buses. Let *their* butts endure the pain, while *mine* sits snug on a soft sofa. Then I realise it's not realistic. I don't have a home — a critical component of the homestay business model. And even if I did, one-star TripAdvisor reviews would be the ruin of me. Guests would complain that I served only omelettes and that when they asked me to clean their room, I told them, "Do it yourself, you lazy sod."

MADURAI

Pyramidal towers crown the four gateways in the fortress-like wall that cocoon the majestic Meenakshi Temple. Each is encrusted with hundreds of statues of multi-armed gods, bug-eyed demons, and mythical beasts; all as vibrant as anime. They're aesthetically awesome — the real sense of the word, not the oh-my-god-those-shoes-are-awesome sense. It dates from millennia ago, from the time that Madurai — once capital of the Pandyan Kingdom — was flush with cash from lucrative trade with China and Greece and Rome. But despite its age, it isn't a lifeless heritage site. Pilgrims flock here now in numbers as great as all those years ago, breathing new life into a temple from an older world.

Inside, strobes of sunlight penetrate loopholes giving dim light to eerie corners. Lotus flowers in garish hues are painted on the high ceilings and sacred symbols are etched in chalk on the slabbed floor. Bats hang at the top of long, high hall-ways lined with columns carved with creatures worn by the years. At the ends of the hallways, men sit on ledges; legs crossed, eyes closed. Their echoed chants mingle with tings and tongs and chimes. And solemn-faced pilgrims pass through ceiling-high, deity-decorated wooden doors that link the many rooms; they take much time to-ing and fro-ing between shrines: pausing to worship, perform rituals, make offerings.

Blackened statues of gods and goddesses stand in dark alcoves lit from within by flickering candles that throw shadows upon hovering faces smeared with sacred ash who hope their softly-muttered prayers and displays of intense dedication will prompt the deities to fulfil their desires. Some of the goddess statues are quite saucy: F-cup breasts and butt cheeks on show. It certainly helps with religion if your maker is sexy, but I'm surprised to see such statues in a temple. It's quite a juxtaposition in a country with such draconian censorship. Beeped words on TV include sex, bottom, condoms. (This book will be the size of a pamphlet by the time it makes it into Indian bookshops.)

In one chamber, a man playing saxophone-sounding tunes on a vuvuzela-looking instrument stands beside an elephant painted with bursts of colour. The elephant bobs about and rocks side to side and lifts and bends each leg by turn in the manner of someone stood on the edge of a dance floor feeling their way into the vibe. People bearing bananas inch nervously towards the elephant. It halts its jiving to take one of the bananas with its trunk and swing it whole into its mouth; then it blesses the giver with a tap on the head.

Outside that chamber is a pool of army-green water; a golden lotus rises from its centre. In ancient times, says Tamil legend, scholars gathered at it to judge the merits of newly-written literature. They threw manuscripts into the water; those that sank were considered inferior while those that floated were worthy of praise. I wish that were the method used for judging the Man Booker Prize: It would be my best chance of winning.

A sign beside the entrance to the temple's inner sanctum states: "Non Hindus are not permitted past this point." I stand on my toes to sneak a peek over the shuffling mass of people with offerings of fruit and flowers in their hands, pressing through the arch into the shadowy chamber. It looks as though there's some high-quality holy shit they're hiding away in there. Unfortunately, I don't know enough about Hinduism to blag my way in. It's too broad to cram for in a five-minute Wikipedia session. There are thirty-six million gods in the Hindu pantheon, and I only know the names of about ten of them. If they quiz me to check I am indeed the Hindu I say I am, the chance of me passing is less than that of Outback Steakhouse opening a branch in this temple.

The Hindu gods I know are the pre-eminent ones — like Shiva and Krishna and Hanuman — believed to control the cosmos. Beyond those are the second-class gods who Hindus pray to for help with day-to-day problems. If a Hindu wants India to win the Cricket World Cup, they might pray to Shiva; but if they want an ill cow to get better, they'll pray to someone lower down the order. "Can't you see I'm busy with the cosmos? Call a vet!" says Shiva to anyone who bothers him with their cow woes. Somewhat confusingly, though, all Hindu gods are actually manifestations of a single god at source — Brahman — from which everything that exists emanates. The reason for the thirty-six million versions of the one is so Brahman can reveal himself to different people in different ways; ways which each person can recognise and understand. It's a smart system, provides a broad religious framework — perfect for the diverse mass market that is India.

I leave thinking that it's the best temple I've ever visited, and I'm not alone in giving it high praise: in 2007, it was one of two hundred monuments worldwide nominated to be one of the New Seven Wonders of the World. It polled impressively, coming in the top thirty. The vote was online, though, and anyone could vote, so its performance was perhaps artificially inflated by vast numbers of Indians backing their own horse in the race — because, of course, to Indians anything Indian-made is the best. But in this particular instance, contrary to my standard stance on the issue, I agree with them.

Outside the temple, women sit threading garlands of flowers; beside them slump beggars, their bony hands outstretched from ragged sleeves — a gesture of habit more than hope. Peddlers and chancers of every age and type have encamped to engage in hopeless, haphazard scheming. By foul means or fair, they try to get their hands on a few rupees — temporarily putting their religion in their back pocket should the means of acquiring those rupees be more foul than fair.

The streets beyond unwind in a tangled coil of colour and commotion. Thousands of little, boxy shops, one after the other, line both sides of Madurai's crisscrossing streets and lanes; a jumble of storefronts selling flotsam worthy of a jumble sale. A lot of jewellers, sometimes several in a row; their windows shining gold. The country is the second largest consumer of gold in the world. The ignorant think India is full of shitty hands, and, well, I suppose it is, but they don't realise there are millions of golden fingers and wrists and necks and ears too.

The temperature is forty-one degrees, and my shirt and jeans are soon drenched with sweat, clinging uncomfortably to me. The time for conceding and wearing shorts is long gone — my legs are too white to bare now. My pasty pins poking out from shorts would resemble prosthetics. People would flick ₹1 coins at me, and I don't want actual cripples going without curry so I can have cool legs. Locals are feeling the heat too, huddled under awnings beside stalls, sweat streaming down their faces as they chug chai and nosh fried snacks — strange choices considering the stifling swelter.

The heat doesn't curdle the mood: Dozens have smiled at me today. That would never happen in the UK, where a smile from a random in the street is rare. Two per week might deviate from the norm and give a slight upturn of the lips. One of those will be on a register. Some locals have done more than smile: a guy on the opposite side of the road shouted hello at me; someone stopped me just to say my shirt was nice; an armed guard sat in a bank asked me to sit with him and share his lunch.

And now a pharmacist has invited me to take a seat behind the counter to drink tea while he goes to another pharmacy to get something for me that he doesn't have in stock. When he returns, we chat for a bit. I tell him I'll next visit Pondicherry, and ask if it's nice there. He does the Indian head wobble — like he's trying to shake water out of his ears. Even now, after months in India, I don't know whether to take this as a yes or a no. My confusion is evident because he adds some words to the wobble.

He says: "Pondicherry is a very nice place; it's so clean there, not like here in Madurai, where it's so dirty. The problem is too many Indians don't take responsibility for where they live. And they don't take care of their own cleanliness either. Only 10% of Indians are educated about this: to clean their face and brush their teeth every day, to go to the toilet in the right place, to not put litter on the floor.

"My hope is that young children will start adopting clean habits. The difficulty is that children learn from adults, and the adults around them are teaching them dirty habits, not clean ones. But I think TV and the internet can help. Now Indian children can see how people live in other countries. If they see foreigners looking clean and living in clean cities, I hope they'll be inspired and learn from that, and India will become clean too."

PONDICHERRY

The overnight sleeper bus from Madurai pulls into Pondicherry at 5.30 am. Despite the wee hour, hordes of auto drivers are at the station hustling: "Come, sir, come. I take you hotel. Best and cheap, sir. Best and cheap. Come, come."

Best and *cheap* are the two words auto drivers love using to describe whatever place they have in mind to drag you off to. They think, and maybe they're right, that those words — "Sir, best and cheap! Best, sir. Cheap!" — are most seductive to foreigners. If I were to take an auto driver up on this seemingly generous offer, there are four options as to where I would end up (percentage chances in brackets):

A place that's the best and also cheap. (0%)

The best place in town but which isn't cheap. (2%)

Somewhere that's cheap but a shithole. (5%)

His friend's place that's neither the best nor cheap. (93%)

On foot, I find my way to the seafront; hundreds and hundreds of locals there on the long, thin strip of beach and the traffic-free promenade that parallels it. Fast-paced strolling with friends or sitting alone — cross-legged, staring meditatively out to sea — are the most popular activities, but feet-touchers and leg-squatters and arm-swingers and star-jumpers and push-uppers are out in force too. One guy is hung upside down — bat-like — from a piece of scaffolding. I may have to sleep like that tonight because my search for accommodation is thus far fruitless.

At a place named Le Cafe, I take a break from searching. I order a croissant and whistle *Frère Jacques* — the only French song I know — while breathing in the breezy air of the Bay of Bengal. Pondicherry's French connection comes from 280 years of French rule, which was time aplenty for them to stamp their mark. Even now, 60 years after the French departed, it still feels like a pukka piece of Paris. The clean, quiet, leafy boulevards have names like Rue Romain Rolland, Goubert Avenue, and Dumas Street. They're lined with grand buildings of colonial pomp that are these days fancy hotels with names like Hotel De L'Orient and Palais De Mahe; and expensive boutiques and pretentious restaurants called Les This and Du That; and cute villas and pastel mansions with flowering balconies. The French vibe, however, only stretches as far as the littered, festering, concrete canal that's five roads back from the seafront; from there, it quickly transitions back to default India. 280 years and the French only fixed up five roads — yet they deny the truth of their slothful stereotype.

I, at last, find a cheap room in the French Quarter; however, I have to make a compromise: staying at a place — New Guest House — associated with Sri Aurobindo Ashram. They dominate Pondicherry, owning 400-plus buildings — shops, banks, schools, restaurants, post offices, guesthouses, travel agencies, printing presses ... (all run by ashram devotees). Most of the buildings the ashram owns are coloured the same distinctive light-grey and are stamped with the same symbol: an overlapping pair of triangles that create a six-point star, inside which is an image of a lotus flower floating on water. It's very cult-like. The ashram, of course, is keen to point out they're not a cult, but the first rule of running one is that you don't call it so. Use other words to disguise yourself, such as society or community or co-operative. That's not to say all groups using those masking words are necessarily operating a cult. Co-op probably is just a supermarket; to be on the safe side, though, I've never signed up for one of their loyalty cards.

New Guest House is an austere, blocky building with a grey, brown, and cream colour scheme. Each of the bedroom doors has attached to the outer side of it a sign that denotes a trait: modesty, intensity, perception ... And each can be padlocked on the outside. Tile mosaics of rainbows and swans add further to the feel of it being an asylum. There are strict, institution-style rules to adhere to, as told to me by the steely, sour-faced woman on reception: silence and discipline must be maintained; no outside food or drink are permitted; the front door is locked at 10.30 pm. The only notable feature of my ascetic room: the greyscale portraits of the ashram founders — Sri Aurobindo and The Mother — hung on the wall at the foot of the bed. Sri Aurobindo looks like Saruman from *The Lord of the Rings*; The Mother like a gypsy fortune teller.

I read some of the pamphlets about Sri Aurobindo, a famous figure in modern Indian history, who died in 1950. He spent his youth living in England and studied at Cambridge University, before returning to India and becoming a leading player in the early stages of the independence movement. (Gandhi, by the way, was also British-educated, and I think the lesson to be learnt for colonial overlords is not to educate the natives; give them only comics and colouring books.) Following a stint in prison — for political reasons, nothing properly naughty — Sri Aurobindo converted from a political figure to a guru and established the ashram in Pondicherry in 1926. After a spiritual revelation led him to withdraw from public view, he handed the running of the ashram over to a French woman known as The Mother — one of the original unwashed, unshaven crusties to arrive in India.

I cross town to visit the ashram: a light-grey mansion rimmed with white that's fringed by high walls. I follow a queue of people dressed in white through the entrance gate into a paved courtyard landscaped with flower beds. In the centre, under the shade of a large tree, is a low-lying, marble tomb in which Sri Aurobindo and The Mother are buried. The silence is intense; there's a palpable mood of reverence. Some are kneeling beside the tomb with expressions of extreme gravity, touching their heads to the marble and murmuring prayers. Others are sat meditating on benches around the courtyard.

I realise the queue is taking me to the tomb for my turn to kneel and pay my respects; so I sidestep out of the queue, but then note there's nowhere for me to go. The way back is blocked with people; the way forward leads only to the tomb. I want to be out the way, over on a bench against the back wall — like the bald foreigner in white pyjamas, gently swaying side to side. There are several flower beds between me and the bench, but they're thin enough to easily leap over. I leap over one and land on a strip of grass.

An old guy — a steward of some kind, also dressed in white — stands from his chair by the entrance and looks at me. He silently mouths something at me, but I can't work out what.

I leap over another flower bed.

The old guy adds hand gestures to his mouthing. I think he wants me to get back in the queue. I try to get across in gestures that I don't want to get back in the queue, that I'm going to sit on a bench next to the beatific baldie.

I leap over another flower bed.

The old guy isn't happy about this. Others are also looking at me now; frowning at the guy wearing black, not white, who's prancing around gesturing. I feel as welcome as an uninvited black man performing unsolicited mime and ballet at a Ku Klux Klan meeting. The old guy starts coming towards me, pushing the limits of how angry a holy man is permitted to look in public. He can't get to me, though, because of all the flower beds between us — which he's more reluctant to jump over than I was.

"Ok, ok, ok," I mouth at him, and decide it's best to abort Mission Sit-On-Bench.

I see a path leading to the bookshop, through which is the exit from the ashram. Between me and the path are another flower bed and a hedge.

I jump over the flower bed, then turn to check on the old guy.

His hands gesture, "No, not that way," and he mouths something unholy and quite frankly rude at me.

I'm on the home straight now, though. I point at the hedge.

He shakes his head.

I nod mine.

His eyes shout, "Don't you dare."

I nod again; then I push through the hedge.

In the bookshop — after picking leaves and twigs off myself — I browse the shelves loaded with titles like *The Problem of Rebirth* and *Hymns to the Mystic Fire* and *Flowers and Their Messages*. On the covers are stock photos of sunsets and mountains. A section from one reads: "Sri Aurobindo and The Mother are not only the explorers of consciousness, they are the builders of a new world. After exploring the outermost frontiers of worlds not unknown to ancient wisdom, they discovered another world, as yet unmapped, which they called Supramental, and which they sought to pull down upon earth."

Sri Aurobindo and The Mother didn't get around to building a new world, but they did manage Auroville — fifteen kilometres from Pondicherry. On reaching the visitor centre at Auroville, I tell the auto driver to wait two hours for me, and that if I'm not back by then to call the British Embassy and order them to get the SAS out in a chopper to rescue me: "Tell them to look for black smoke. I've swallowed a lighter which I can shit out and use to set fire to my flip-flops."

It's plush and trendy inside the visitor centre and the people working here are all sweetness and light. Scientologists, I suspect, do the same with their visitor centres: it's free hugs and ice cream until you've signed the form, then you're carted off to a subterranean bunker in the desert for a lifetime of polishing Cruise's shoes. Display boards explain that Auroville isn't one town but a network of a hundred small sites and communities scattered across forested grounds, and that there are about 2,500 permanent residents, from a few dozen countries, plus a number of long-term visitors, who come to Auroville to volunteer for months at a time. The application process to become an Aurovillian takes two years and requires applicants to prove they are self-sustainable and dedicated to the cause. A committee called Entry Services makes the final decision.

The centrepiece of Auroville is the Matrimandir (meaning "Temple of The Mother") — a sphere covered with hundreds of golden discs, that from photos in the visitor centre bears more than a passing resemblance to a massive Ferrero Rocher. Visitors are only allowed to see it after watching a propaganda video about Auroville and The Mother's vision for it. Instrumental music backs the ten-minute video; a droning, hypnotic voice preaches over it. I poke myself in the eye now and then to prevent any brainwashing trickery they may be trying.

Having watched the video, I get a Matrimandir pass from a hippie woman sat on a chair — a finger pressed on either side of her head. I walk to it along a red-dust path through woodlands, being directed by glassy-eyed people in pyjama-like uniforms who are stood around humming. When a van with tinted windows, and Sri Aurobindo's symbol stuck on its side, drives slowly past me, I worry it's scouting for sceptics, so I adopt a stupefied expression and mumble, "I love Mummy."

The Matrimandir is quite a sight: a golden sphere encircled by twelve sandstone lotus petals. Manicured gardens surround it — a space Aurovillians call "Peace". Twenty metres away is as close as I can get. To go in you have to lodge in Auroville several days and convince a gatekeeper that you want to enter to "find your consciousness". At the visitor centre, though, was an exhibit detailing what's inside the Matrimandir: "The spacious inner chamber is completely white, with white marble walls and white carpeting. In the centre sits a crystal globe which suffuses a ray of guided sunlight that falls on it through an opening at the apex of the sphere."

Beside the Matrimandir is an amphitheatre, where a few times a year a fire is lit at dawn and Aurovillians gather for collective meditation. In front of the amphitheatre, on top of a small mound, is a white urn; inside it is the Auroville Charter, handwritten by The Mother. The first statement of the charter is: "To live in Auroville, one must be the willing servitor of the Divine Consciousness."

Definitely sounds culty ... Were I to have a daughter — like Aoise — who said she was coming to live here, I'd say, "Pumpkin, you know I love you, and I know I said I'd always support your choices in life, but if you go there, you're a fuckwit."

HYDERABAD

The 1591-built Charminar, with its chunky arches and towering minarets, marks the centre of Hyderabad. It overlooks the 10,000-capacity Mecca Masjid: the second largest mosque in India, and among the largest in the world. In the area around — known as the Old City — burqa-wearers shuffle between Indo-Islamic-styled buildings scrawled with Urdu script and flying crescent-and-star flags. This Islamisation is a consequence of successive Islamic dynasties ruling the city — once capital of an eponymous princely state; now capital of a state called Telangana — between 1724 and 1948.

In the 1900s, it was the richest state in the country; and in 1937, say *Time*, its ruler was the richest man in the world. Even a decade after that — well into the 1940s — the state had an income equal to that of Belgium. Then the bottom fell out of Hyderabad. It wanted to become independent from India following the country's break from Britain in 1947, but the Hindu-majority government said no. With its finances divvied up and dispersed, and the government neglecting the state in favour of Hindu-majority ones, the once grand city of Hyderabad slid into decay and disrepair. Only lingering hints of luxury are left, glimpses of grandeur amid rubble and grime. Once elegant facades are cracked, smeared, crumbled — or even gone without a trace. It's impossible to reconcile the Hyderabad of the decadent dynasties of before — a place that awed foreign visitors — with the congested urban abyss that is Hyderabad today. The chasm between the two visions is unbridgeable.

I make my way — pushed, elbowed, shouldered — through the chaotic, winding lanes of the centuries-old bazaars that radiate from the Charminar, among too many — far too many — people and autos and cars. The throngs browse goat meat hanging on hooks and stalls of sparkly bracelets, and buy fusty figs and manky mangoes from grubby sellers pushing wooden carts. The air is foul, a noxious treacle of fumes and dust, and all over is a pissy whiff from phallus waterfalls. I feel the toxins filling my lungs, sickening them the way sewage has poisoned the city's fetid Musi River.

The fumes are so thick because it's a super-sized city — the fourth largest in India — without a metro. One is in the process of being built but is already two years behind schedule and isn't expected to be completed for another two years at least. The dust is mostly from extensive construction; all around, new bricks being added to new buildings climbing steadily skywards. But some of it's from existing buildings disintegrating, a result of being shoddily put up like the new ones are. In Kolkata, a couple of months ago, a flyover collapsed and killed dozens of people. It was only the latest episode in a tragic series of similar incidents.

Despite the widespread construction in Hyderabad, 1.5 million of the city's 7 million population still don't have a home — at least not a proper home. They live in one of the 1,500 slums in the city. I pass some of these squalid, shambolic settlements, wreathed in smoke from smouldering garbage fires, as I walk along a traffic-jammed four-lane carriageway. Some of the "homes" within are flimsy tent-like shelters: sheets of tarpaulin and threadbare blankets draped over crooked, fragile frames. Others look more permanent, shack-like: roped and taped and nailed scraps of wood, metal, plastic, cardboard. All are pitiful patchworks of brokenness. Their counterparts in Mumbai's Dharavi slum are comfortable lodgings in comparison. The faces of the inhabitants are creased with misery. Brown faces are black with grime; tattered clothes sag off wasted bodies. Women hold crying babies to their chest, trying to shield their eyes from the smoke, their ears from the traffic. One squats beside a flow of filth, making chapattis over a fire of broken twigs and assorted trash. Another lays in the dirt, using a rag over a brick as a pillow.

Hyderabadis lucky enough not to live in a slum mostly reside in dreary concrete blocks that combine to create a shabby sprawl. As I walk across it, I find myself checking over my shoulder for the first time since Delhi. At one point, a guy steps towards me and flips something up and out at me from his side. I jerk back, thinking the shiny, black object to be a knife or gun. It's not; it's a pair of centre-folding sunglasses he's trying to sell. None of the many stares I receive conclude with nods or waves or smiles. I read harshness and bitterness on the staring faces, even on the young ones. I try not to take it personally, tell myself it's their default expression, but some of the scornful stares feel as though they're just for me: dirty looks at the cleanest one out. For these are a scruffy, filthy bunch — the scruffiest and filthiest yet. It's not only the city that's been left to languish but its people too.

I see no foreign faces, not a single hippie. They're off "finding themselves" in traveller-friendly enclaves that stock croissants and wheatgrass shots. It's easy to be calm and smiley sat on a yoga mat in Rishikesh or looking at a crystal ball in Auroville; less so among the horrors of Hyderabad. Those that claim money and possessions are obstacles to happiness should come here, face to face with countless people who have almost none of either. They would see these people could hardly be further from happiness. India ranked 118 out of 156 countries in the latest *World Happiness Report* published by the United Nations. Hyderabadis, I suspect, would have ranked their country even lower.

Walking further, I pass dingy, charred workshops ranging in size from that of a garage to that of an ensuite bathroom. Red fires burn, blue sparks fly, black hands work: sawing and welding and hammering. The hunched bodies and grimaced faces baring missing and reddened teeth look almost orc-like. There isn't enough such work in India, where the masses would be keen to take on the type of low-skilled, labour-intensive manufacturing jobs that powered China's rise. For decades, manufacturing as a percentage of India's GDP has plateaued in the mid-teens. This is far below not only China but many other Asian countries too.

India does, though, have the edge over China on IT. Half the world's outsourced IT services come from India, and it's an industry that accounts for a fifth of the country's exports. Hyderabad competes with Bangalore for the crown of India's IT capital, earning itself the nickname "Cyberabad". Based on that, before coming here, I expected a cutting-edge city, an up-and-coming Singapore. But Singapore is light years ahead of Hyderabad. If Singapore were a PS4, Hyderabad would be Pong. Google and Microsoft have their Indian headquarters in Hyderabad; Facebook, IBM, and Dell have set up camp too. All are on the outskirts of the city in glass buildings set in landscaped grounds behind high walls — to keep the real Hyderabad at bay.

Google-and-their-like operate on tax breaks and make

huge profits. And make no mistake that profits are what brought those companies — and thousands more like them — to India. They aren't here out of goodwill, as a charitable act. Foreign companies typically pay Indians salaries that are a quarter or less — often much less — than those paid to equivalent workers in their country. An oversupply of human capital in India means this will long be the case. It creates an Indian economic paradox: its poor are its wealth. The economy is driven by them, would fail without them.

I give up walking: too much of a grim sameness, too many pavements not yet paved. The auto I wave down tells me he knows where I want to go. He says, "Ok, I know. In, in, in. ₹150." Then he pulls over two minutes later to ask someone to translate for him where I want to go. Now he actually knows where I want to go, the dickhead doubles the price. He drives like a getaway driver but we get nowhere fast because of the traffic. A dozen-plus times he beeps in the next five minutes — each time unnecessarily. Then we pull over again: the brake lever is broken. He gets out, fiddles with some pliers, then holds up a frayed cable: "No problem," he says. "I fix."

While he's faffing around, three generations of a beggar family — a girl, a woman, a grannie — storm me. Arms reach in at me from both sides of the auto; the gropers each clad in black, wearing a headscarf. Moans and groans utter from their deathly expressions. They should quit begging, get a job at a ghost train: they've got the looks, the moves, the noises.

The auto drops me off at the wrong place. I can't be arsed to argue; I just want rid of him. I hate auto drivers. Cunts. *All* of them. India has turned me into a vehiclist — someone who judges a person not by the content of their character but by the vehicle they drive.

KOLKATA

Kolkata — or Calcutta, as it was called before — served as the capital of British-held India until 1911. For more than a century, it was the political and economic powerhouse of India, and became one of the world's wealthiest cities. A construction spree in its heyday resulted in buildings as grand and exquisite as those in Victorian London: Fort William, Marble Palace, Writers' Building, St Paul's Cathedral, General Post Office — these and others aren't only fit for The Strand and Trafalgar Square but look as though they were transplanted from there. The clearest statement that the British thought they were here to stay is the imperious Victoria Memorial. The bulbous-domed, mint-white marble hall stands regally among the manicured greenery of an expansive estate. No one thinking themselves a mere tenant would have bothered with such grandiosity.

Beyond the ornamental imprints of the Raj, trams clank along the same clogged roads as sixties-style yellow taxis. Psychedelic buses sporting swastikas and spewing fumes screech to halts to burp out sardines; their conductors hang as far out the sweatboxes as possible, folded notes between each knuckle of each hand, like origami Wolverines ready to inflict paper cuts on fare evaders. Rickety rickshaws are pulled — not cycled — by barefooted blokes performing the role of a horse; they grin when getting a customer, grimace when setting off at a lame gallop, pulling their wagon-wheeled contraptions behind them. Bags, boxes, baskets, and bundles balanced on heads stream every which way from the central SS Hogg Market; outside its skewed red-brick walls, feathers fly as frantically squawking chickens are pulled feet-first from poop-covered wicker cages and killed on the spot with a neck-breaking flick of the wrist. Blood from the chickens and the flapping fish gutted nearby runs thick in the gutter. Rats and cats and cows and crows forage the filth. Other crows crowd chucked carton trays, pecking the rotting remnants of broken eggs. The foul smell fuses with the whiff of warm, stale piss from a row of outdoor urinals and raw shit spilling from a sewer. Metres away, a dainty woman in a bright sari sells cucumbers from a sack; she stands amid the muck like a lotus in a muddy pond. Inside the market's muggy, mouldering meat hall, men wearing holey vests sit on tree stump stools chopping bloody joints on stone slabs with stained knives. Cigarettes hang from their mouths; sweat-dripped fringes cling to their glistening foreheads. Birds swoop from the scaf-fold-propped ceiling to compete with scavenging dogs for discarded scraps. At street kitchens around the market, cardamom, cumin, and chilli perfume the air, providing passing respite to tortured nostrils. Diners sit sweltering beneath ripped awnings and threadbare canopies eating dishes tastier than you'll find at your local Taj in a setting worse than your local tip.

Beyond the market, everywhere I wander I see scenes of squalor, depictions of deprivation. It's a relentless tapestry of poverty, worse than I've seen anywhere else in India. The destitute are etched into street after street of deep-seated urban decay. Streets lined with bleak buildings blackened by grime and so caked with dirt it appears to be the glue holding together the bowed bricks and peeled plaster and glassless windows. The fractured pavements teem with encampments: canvases tied to railings and cack-handed structures made of waste items. The dwellers sleep in them, cook beside them, toilet behind them. Only inches away, traffic and people stream past, peering into the intimacy of home life lived publicly. Countless others inhabit hovels beside train tracks; so close they could leap from their door onto a passing train. In the eighties, Rajiv Gandhi — Indian Prime Minister at the time — called Kolkata a "dying city". It's since died and decomposed. The resurrection has yet to come. What was once the London of the East is now not even the Luton of the East. Yet still people migrate here: the displaced, the desperate. Kolkata's population has nearly doubled over the past few decades.

The characters on this crumbled, chaotic canvas are fraught and frenetic, competing fiercely among themselves for survival. It's *Lord of the Flies* meets musical chairs. Sometimes it boils over: I see three fistfights in an hour. For some, it's too much — the city has felled them — and as I walk I wince at the wounds of the human wreckage, at the cuts, boils, and sores scored on the sickly skin of lame limbs, and at the casualties riddled with illness, plagued by disease. Feeble figures with faces filthed by hardship hover on every street, and emaciated, goggle-eyed junkies crouch over burning spoons or inhale vapour from plastic bags. Dolled-up prostitutes wrapped in coloured shawls emerge then vanish into darkened doorways. A pimp tells me, "Only ₹200." Skeletal children gather near me and make pleas of hunger; gesturing to their mouths, rubbing their tummies. Others stand alone, looking lost in the world: emblems of abjectness blinking sorrowfully; their eyes dulled by stunted growth, suffocated dreams, smothered hopes. Babies sleep on unwashed blankets and cardboard scraps near kerbs; others are used as tools by begging women. "Money, money, my baby," I get bawled at me. One says she wants the money to buy milk powder. I ask her how much. "₹400," she says. She's taking the piss — that's way too much. "What have you given birth to?" I say, brushing her off. "A baby fucking elephant?!"

The ubiquity of suffering in this country has made me blasé about it. 270 million Indians live below the poverty line, and it feels as though I've personally met all of them, that each has requested ₹10 from me. I don't hold much hope for them. Of those pitied — the at-war and the starving, the tyrannised and the persecuted — the poverty-stricken are bottom of the list. Just being poor — even the most abject life-long variety — isn't sufficient to be news. Blanked by the media, and thus by the public, they remain nameless and faceless, left to perish without hope of salvation. Or with, maybe, a single hope: a war. Those fleeing a country with nothing being somehow regarded a worthier cause than those with nothing but a country to call home — despite not having a home in that country and no prospect of ever having one. The Indian government isn't oblivious to its poverty problem, and makes something of an effort, but the norm is half-baked policies half-implemented. Radical projects to help the poor get loudly announced then later quietly shelved. First-world ambitions are chased while third-world problems remain.

Some Indians are pleased the plight of their poor isn't publicised and complain about foreigners talking of poverty in their country. "It's patronising and hypocritical," they say. "There are poor people in every country." Which is true. But while there's relative poverty in the West, of the absolute poverty suffered in India, endured like a cruel whip until a premature death, there's very little — or even none. In the UK, even the poorest of the poor have a roof over their head, their health tended to, their minds schooled. And while there are plenty of poor in the West, and a chasm between them and the rich, the majority fall somewhere in the middle. In India, the majority fall at the poor end of the spectrum — and the majority of those at the extremity of it. To not talk about them — the majority — would be negligent. The prosperous twenty-first century India the middle and upper classes talk of does exist — if you look upwards at the buildings rising. At the foot of those buildings, though, are slumped a quarter of a billion paupers, catatonically miserable as the economic miracle passes them by. Look up, you see riches; look down, you see horrors.

None more so than the woman laid on her back on the pavement ahead. As I get closer, I see the dirt daubed on her shift. I realise it's not dirt: she's coated in flies.

I get closer still, half a metre away. *Her face; oh, her fucking face.* It's half missing. The flesh on the right side is gone: from her eye to her cheek to her lips to her chin to her throat.

I pass her in what feels like slow motion but must only be a second. I walk on five metres, shaken; then I stop and look behind: People walk past her and on past me; they're undisturbed, unconcerned.

Wait, what? No ... *Surely not?* But ... *Fuck!* Her leg just moved. Only a twitch but it moved. *Is she not yet dead? If she, for fuck's sake, still alive?!*

I cross the road and backtrack to stand opposite where she is but railings and a lamppost block a clear view of her. So I walk further down the street then cross the road again. After psyching myself up, I start a second walk by: I pass her and see the festered face again and I'm sickened further by the slight rise and fall of her barely-covered bony chest.

She's not dead.

The guy just ahead of me slows and looks back; he looks at the woman, then up at me. "Dead," he says.

"But, but ... she's not dead," I say. "She's still breathing."

He shrugs and walks on.

I walk on too and leave the scene behind. The scene, however, won't leave my mind. For kilometres, I walk in a daze, trying to get away; on and on through the dying city, where death haunts the streets, assails the living.

Then I slow, then I pause ...

And then I turn — turn to walk back to her. I don't know why. Not to save her — she's too far gone. Possibly to know how long she'll be left there. Perhaps to be with her for her final breath. Maybe to finish her off, to end her pain.

But I can't find my way back to her. Too spun out after leaving the scene, I'm unable to trace a return. So she's left there alone to die. One of too many in this city, in this country, who are uncared for, unwanted, unloved — forgotten by everybody.

THE END

The land of the English aristocracy is almost entirely PRIVATE. What happens if you go over the walls and off the paths and stroll around that land? What happens if you take a tent with you and spend a night on that land? Mark finds out in this book about trespass, about wild camping, about dukes.

www.gonzo.schule/duchyland

BELGRAVE AVENUE

The Duke of Westminster is, this very moment, at Charles's coronation; he's carrying a royal flag — a VIP role — as he leads Charles's and the Not-Quite-Queen's procession from Buckingham Palace to Westminster Abbey. He's there, and I'm here: outside his manor — which is in Cheshire.

In front of me is an imposing, black gate with golden detailing — pillars on either side of it, stone hounds atop them. A sign yells, "PRIVATE". To the right, on the other side of the gate, is an olde red-brick building — Belgrave Lodge. Far down the drive, an obelisk stands tall, and far behind the obelisk is the Big House.

To the side of the grand gate is a little stone wall — so

little that I could step over; I wouldn't even need to climb. And at the far left side of that little stone wall is a little white gate — is it locked? No. I open it, walk in ... I start along the driveway — Belgrave Avenue — an arrow-straight gauntlet bordered by thick woods. I wonder: Has anyone *ever* arrived by bus (the No.1 from Chester to Wrexham, which I got off after twenty minutes) and then *walked* along this drive? No, not likely.

You might think: *That's his drive! You shouldn't go down there!* But I could walk a couple of kilometres along his drive and still not know what cars are parked outside his house. I won't go all the way down to his house — though, even if I did, would that be so wrong? He's allowed to walk down anyone else's driveway, right? If he wished, Hugh Grosvenor — that's his real name, this duke — he could walk down *your* drive and knock on *your* door.

He knows I'm coming: I sent an email last week ...

"I accept my invitation to visit you. I'll arrive on foot and stay in a tiny green tent. I'll wander around a little to see what you're doing with all that land. But fear not, I come in peace, and I won't be a nuisance during my stay. I'm sure you'll know that trespass isn't a criminal offence. Aggravated trespass is, but I won't be doing any aggravating while I'm with you. A civil offence is what trespass is, and you may thus wish to sue me for this heinous misdemeanour. That's okay — you can do that. You can also phone the police; technically, they shouldn't come, what with trespass not being a crime and me being a finely-behaved trespasser, but I understand that if you make the call, they likely will come. That's okay — you can do that."

A guy replied: Dobbs — Head of Family Office & Rural

Estates. He said, "We don't condone trespass", but he also said that if I'm coming anyway, let him know when, and he'll tell me somewhere "safe" that I can pitch the tent. Very nice of him — or, at least, so it seemed ... But I didn't email him back because it could also be a trap. The estate is so large that if they don't know when I'm coming or from which direction, it's impossible to keep me out. But if they know when I'm coming and where I'll enter, a crack squad of ex-paratroopers might pounce. That's the sort of thing that this duke can afford. He's worth nearly £10 billion — 11th on *The Sunday Times* Rich List 2023.

Halfway along the drive from the gate, I turn off it into Kennel Wood. I'm on a tyred track, but it's clear people don't come in these woods often: the track is really overgrown; no one could have driven down here for months. It's dense with trees and shrubs; a few soupy ponds. Some dirty-looking mushrooms there, which I won't be foraging, as I'm well stocked with Tesco Luxury Fruit & Nut Mix. Loads of stinging nettles — *ah*, *ooh*, *ouch* — and lots of thorns scragging my skinny jeans. I had to bin the Converse from last time — they were ruined. I was down to flip-flops or riding boots or Chelsea boots. I went for Chelsea boots — black, suede. Though unsuitable for the countryside, they're classy. If I meet someone, what will they make of a trespasser who looks like this? These boots, these jeans, these shades ... If I'm better dressed than them, better smelling than them, how will they deal with that? Plus, I got a dictaphone, a snazzy, little Sony. Stick that in their face makes me look like a pro. "Anything *you* say may be used in evidence against *you*." Give them a card — "Yes, that *is* a German domain ..." — and ask *them* what *they're* doing. That will melt their brain; pure Jedi shit.

I roam the woods, a roundabout route, crunching foot-steps, brambles, thorns — *argh*, *ouch*, *argh* — and I come out on an opening ... There are grimy plastic containers; diesel in them, I guess. Bits of crap and junk all over the ground: green netting, polystyrene, red-and-white tape, blue rope, a Fudge wrapper, bottle tops ... At the edge of the woods is a field, a field in which they're growing something. Tractor tracks across it; there always is; there's no other way to farm a field. To cross this field, along the margins or following the tractor tracks, and damage nothing is simple. You don't need to be a farmer to know how to cross a field; you can just see it like you can see where and when to cross a road. It just takes a smidge of common sense that anyone older than six has.

I cross that field, then more fields ... Left, over there, the obelisk, and to the right of that, a gothic clocktower — part of Eaton Hall, I think. An orange digger there, paused in motion from Friday. A dog barking far off and the smell of manure, the stuff piled up ... I come to a runway. Hugh could later land his jet here, but I bet he stays in London, spends the night in Mayfair or Belgravia. He owns most of those places. In a *Guardian* article on the most expensive streets in the UK, two of the top five are Grosvenor Square, Mayfair (average house price: £23.5 million) and Grosvenor Crescent, Belgravia (£15.4 million).

Hugh's website says, "The Grosvenor family ancestry can be traced back almost 1,000 years, while its association with London property began over 340 years ago — in 1677 — when land to the west of the City of London came into the family following the marriage of Sir Thomas Grosvenor to Mary Davies." Which is true but is vague on detail. It doesn't mention, for example, that 21-year-old Thomas Grosvenor married Mary Davies when she was 12. That's not a typo: T-W-E-L-V-E. That's how that land in London was acquired.

Hugh's website says, as well, that they trace their ancestry to Gilbert le Grosveneur, who came to England with William the Conqueror. But it seemed from my Sherlocking that Hugh d'Avranches, the 1st Earl of Chester, is the source, and I asked ChatGPT to confirm that, as there were conflicting histories; it said: "The Grosvenor family, including the current Duke of Westminster, can trace their ancestry back to Hugh d'Avranches."

So why wouldn't the Grosvenors say that? Why big up boring Gilbert — thought to be the nephew of Hugh d'Avranches, and who seems historically inconsequential — when they could go large on d'Avranches?

Well, this is the Encyclopedia Britannica entry for Hugh d'Avranches ... "Hugh d'Avranches, the 1st Earl of Chester, also called Hugh The Fat ... Companion of William the Conqueror, who made him Earl of Chester in 1071 ..."

Hugh The Fat in French is Hugh Le Gros ... Interesting, right? *Gros* — *Gros*venor ... Bit of a goddamn coincidence that. Hugh, so the story goes, was so obese he could hardly walk. Yes, not really an ancestor you'd want to publicise.

This land I'm on now is a direct result of that obese French invader. It's in the *Domesday Book*: "Eaton, Cheshire: Owner, 1086: Earl Hugh of Chester." It was seized from someone and given, for free, to Hugh The Fat, then passed on and on and on from then until now, until this Hugh today.

I'm now on a lane through Park Plantation on my way to Duck Wood, walking to the area where I think, based on my scouting of the estate on the OS map, I want to pitch up ... Untamed forest edges the lane, and I inhale the fresh, spring greenness, listen to the soothing birdsong ... I turn onto a muddy track taking me through woodland to Oxleisure Pool; then out the woods and into a meadow: long grass, daisies and dandelions, buttercups and purple wildflowers, butterflies and birds. They're clearly not doing anything with this land here, though maybe animals graze it time to time. In his email, Dobbs mentioned livestock, but I've not seen a single sheep or cow, not even a rabbit or a deer ... Oxleisure Pool is a pretty lake; a few swans in there. Another lovely lake is near it, and the River Dee runs close behind that lake, and over the river is Aldford — a whole village owned by Hugh.

The meadows around these lakes are much, much larger than Grosvenor Park in the middle of Chester, which I went to ... Last night, I stayed in Chester. I stayed at a guesthouse there on a lane called Grosvenor Place, and that lane came off a road called Grosvenor Street, on which is the Grosvenor Museum — and also the Magistrates Court, which I might end up in if charged with aggravated trespass. At the end of Grosvenor Street is Grosvenor Roundabout, and on the other side of Grosvenor Roundabout is Grosvenor Road, where is the Crown Court — to end up there, I'd have to be very, very bloody naughty. Go a little along Grosvenor Road, you cross Grosvenor Bridge ... The other end of Grosvenor Street, en route to Grosvenor Park, is Grosvenor Shopping Centre; and in Grosvenor Park is a Sicilian marble statue of Richard Grosvenor, 2nd Marquess of Westminster, robed and looking like a Roman emperor. The Grosvenors gifted that park to the plebs; they did that in 1867. *Nice!* But the population of Chester has boomed since then: In 1801, Chester had a population of 15,000. In 1901, the population had reached 38,000. It's now 88,000. The park is the same size (20 acres) as it was, but many more people must share it. And, anyway, what's 20 acres out of 11,000 acres, which is the size of this estate? 0.2% is what it is. And this estate is only some of Hugh's rural land. He also has the 23,000-acre Abbeystead Estate in Lancashire, and Reay Forest Estate in Scotland — 96,000 acres — and 37,000 acres near Cordoba in southern Spain, and ...

I drop my bag in the meadow beside Oxleisure Pool, and I lay on my back, relax. The sun is breaking through on what's been an overcast, windy day. I'm surrounded by dandelions, lady's bedstraw, cow parsley; at one with nature in this charming meadow. A yellow butterfly flutters past, and bees buzz from flower to flower. A church — one in Aldford — bongs over the birdsong: *Bong. Bong. Bong.* This is it for today: I'll take it easy right here in this lovely meadow, this meadow that is, after all, really the point of roaming, to discover and savour places like this ... At Huddleton Estate, I got to see off the paths, see what was "PRIVATE", and I saw, and I enjoyed, a glut of joyous spaces like this one right here. Across those 2,000 acres, I could, whenever I wished, skip about naked chasing butterflies. *I* could, but 99.9999999% of people *couldn't*. If they were caught chasing butterflies *au naturel*, there would be a fuss, even though Mother Nature cared not whether it was them doing it or me. While on that estate, I realised that we're being rationed the countryside unnecessarily, realised there was plenty of unused countryside available for people to escape the noise, the hustle, the queues, the sirens, the mad dogs ... An abundance of countryside to escape to that we're for no good reason barred from.

I'll just chill for now, won't put up the tent yet, even though it's unlikely that anyone will come and rant at me: The nearest building, I think, is Black & White Cottages — as the OS map calls them — half a kilometre away, and it's a Saturday today, so aside from the coronation, people on estates just don't work on Saturdays anyway. Farmers need days off, gamekeepers too, and forestry workers, and they just do Monday to Friday because why not? Everyone at Huddleton Estate did that, and I understood that was typical on these sorts of estates. 07:00 til 16:00 was the shift they did year-round there. I'll wait until past 18:00 until I pitch the tent, as if I put it up now and someone does collar me, they'll know where I am and could terrorise me through the night. That's what I'd do if I were them: I'd come back in the night making ghost noises, spraying manure on the tent — teach the cheeky bastard a lesson.

I pick up a little phone signal and watch a video about the loons that have been camping outside Buckingham Palace and along The Mall for days, the poor and the posh alike there for a front-row seat at the royal pantomime. It's like an upbeat refugee camp with Prosecco and PG Tips. A Geordie in a Pound Shop tiara says, "I'm like a five-year-old before Christmas, waiting to open my presents."

Others have taken the opposite stance: there have been arrests of anti-monarchists protesting earlier today. *BBC News* says ...

> "Dozens of people have been arrested during the King's coronation ... Accusations of heavy-handed enforcement started early on Saturday when the Chief Executive of anti-monarchist campaign group Republic — Graham Smith — was arrested at a protest in Trafalgar Square. Footage showed protesters in 'Not My King' t-shirts being detained ... 'The reports of people being arrested for peacefully protesting the coronation are incredibly alarming,' said Human Rights Watch UK director Yasmine Ahmed. 'This is something you would expect to see in Moscow, not London.'"

They hadn't really done anything, it seems; they were simply standing in the street, yelling. I can't be bothered with that. No one listens to people yelling in the street. If I hear someone yelling in the street, my instinct is to take the other side of whatever they're yelling about. As for the Insulate Britain crew glueing themselves to highways ... no, screw them — idiots. The same goes for that business with throwing orange powder on a snooker table at the World Championship in Sheffield, which some Just Stop Oil fool did the other week — in a first-round match, not even the final. That made me want to buy oil — buy it, then pour it down the sink. A protest should be directly linked to the cause you're protesting for. The Animal Rising stunt at the Grand National, fair enough — horses die in the Grand National, so try and stop the Grand National. 118 people arrested there for "criminal damage and public nuisance offences". The result? The race started fourteen minutes late — so fair enough, though pointless. But this, this now ... I wanted to come on this land, and I have done; and I've been here for hours, and I'll sleep here tonight, enjoying myself. If I was just standing outside the front gate, yelling ... waste of time. Hugh's driveway is so damn long that no one would even hear me.

A choir of birds wakes me. I laze a little, dine on nuts for breakfast. A splodge of Molton Brown under my armpits instead of a shower, then I pack up ...

A layer of mist is over the dewy meadow, and I cross it under the morning's golden glow ... I come to a road: I could turn right to reach Aldford Lodge and, from there, leave over Iron Bridge to Aldford — that would be the easy way out. But I'll turn left: walk up to and past the obelisk, and then exit via a back entrance into Eccleston — another village owned by Hugh — where I can walk down Eaton Road into Chester. That route, from here into Eccleston, is about 4 km — right through the centre of the estate.

I walk the road through meadowy pastures, see some geese, a pheasant; I hear a woodpecker, see one of those lodges that I saw at the front gate ... A black railing fence ahead, a gate; I could climb that fence if I need to but let's see if the gate is open: Yes, it's open ... I stay on the road, pass majestic trees; to the right, over long grass and wildflowers blanketed with wispy mist, is the gothic clocktower ... I come to a crossroads: in the centre is an island of grass, the red-tinged obelisk rising to a tapered point; on one side of it is a blue circle within a stone wreath, and within the circle is a medieval golden gate.

Behind the obelisk is the final stretch of driveway to the Big House; a flag — too far away for me to see the design — flies on a pole from its roof. Hugh's actual garden, his super-manicured private garden — I can see from the OS map — stretches for at least a hundred metres *behind* the Big House. So what's all this *in front* of the Big House? A vast open space, parkland unfurling into the distance. It's not landscaped as Grosvenor Park in Chester is, there are no flowerbeds, but it's a much larger space here, far, far so, much larger than the meadows around Oxleisure Pool, far larger than those; several golf courses could easily fit in this "PRIVATE" parkland.

The sun is burning bright and clear now, chasing off the last of the mist. The road bends around a cricket pitch — a white pavilion on the far side of it, and, to the right, I see more lodges. A few deer over there, beside the cricket pitch; the first deer I've seen, the first animals besides birds ... I see a car on the move up ahead: Is it coming this way? ... No ... A couple now going the other way, and they must both have seen me, but neither seems to give a toss. From that distance, though, they can't see my face; I could be anyone, and that anyone is more likely to be someone who works on the estate than a random Brummie.

A gate now, and this one is shut; a black, iron gate, high and ornate and spiked on top. The gate is decorated with golden crowns, golden sheaves, golden Ws; and a blue-and-gold coat of arms with the words "*Virtus Non Stemma*" —

Virtue Not Ancestry, the Grosvenor family motto. I push the gate, but it won't open; I fiddle with it, see if there's any latch, but there's not, so I take to the grass beside the gate, follow along the fence, see how far it goes, see if there's a better place to climb, somewhere further from the road — the road I've just seen three cars drive along. Twenty metres from the gate, the metal fence is only a bit over waist-high; I can climb that easily. I lob my bag over, then leap over myself.

Ah, here's another car now, and this one looks like it's coming for me ... Looks like there's a camera on top of it; a black Range Rover it is. Yeah, it's definitely coming for me ...

As I walk back onto and along the road, that car drives through the gate that I couldn't get through. It comes up behind, driving slowly ... Right behind me now, then alongside me ... "You ok?" he says, staying inside the car — a stocky middle-aged meathead with a crew cut; he wears black, has a body-cam on a stab vest.

"Yeah, good."

Then, oddly, he asks the same thing again: "You ok, yeah?"

"Yep." And I stick the dictaphone through the window. "Anything you say may be ..."

"Ok." And I expect him to maybe ask something, like, I don't know, what the heck I'm doing, but he doesn't ... He doesn't ask anything.

"Here's my card," I say, and I hand it through the window. "Yes, .schule, that *is* a German domain ..."

"Ok."

And that's it.

I carry on walking, and he hovers behind in the car.

As I stroll through the succulent parkland, I wonder why that bloke hasn't questioned me more — or, in fact, at all. I wonder if Dobbs put out a memo about me ... "NOTE: A prat has invited himself to visit us. Say nothing to this prat." As I ponder that, the guy drives past me and off down the road.

I see him again standing beside the gate that leads into the village of Eccleston. He's already opened the gate for me by the time I reach it. He doesn't say anything. I ask if Dobbs told him I was coming, but he says not; he doesn't even know who Dobbs is. I walk out, and he locks the gate after me.

FOOTLOOSE
MARK WALTERS

Backpacking overland across Asia, Mark takes buses and trains and boats from Australia to Azerbaijan. He catches a cargo ship across the Indian Ocean, risks a dicey gauntlet of terrorists and Chinese tanks, has beers with a naked ex-Soviet officer in Kazakhstan ...

www.gonzo.schule/footloose

INDIAN OCEAN

Fremantle is a 25-minute train ride from Perth. At the entrance to its North Quay Harbour, a queue of trucks wait. I walk past them, past the eyes of the drivers looking down at the odd fella in flip-flops. I sit in the security gatehouse, waiting for them to check my story — my story of riding a freighter to Singapore. I get the all-clear, and a security guard drives me to one of the ships, drives me past giant cranes, past thousands of containers, past men in yellow jackets buzzing around. I climb steep metal stairs onto the deck, from where a Filipino bloke — Bernardo — takes me to a seven-floor structure towards the back of the ship that spans almost its width;

in it are offices, bedrooms, dining rooms. My room is one of a few kept spare for journeys that require extra crew. It has a lounge, bedroom, and bathroom, and is furnished like a suite at a 3-star hotel. A TV, a DVD player, and a HiFi system (with tape deck). And towels: *Three! Decadence!* Everything strapped in place, including an artificial potted plant in the corner — the straps to stop things falling in rough seas. Other signs that life at sea might not be smooth: A yellow hard hat and life jacket hang on wall hooks, and on a table is a large black holdall, a white label stitched onto it: "Solas smart suit type 2a. An insulated immersion suit / anti-exposure suit. Made in Scunthorpe."

Bernardo gives me an information booklet, tells me to wait in my room, then leaves. The booklet looks like it was created in the mid-nineties when clip art was cutting edge and anyone with Microsoft Publisher was a graphic designer. Images used include bananas, dancers, flowers — none have any relevance to the text. I learn that the ship is called MSC Uganda (but is German, not Ugandan). It's 294 metres long; it can hold 4,545 shipping containers. Those stats make it sound like a beast, yet it's one of the smallest ships here.

I wait, watch the cranes, snooze for a while, and slowly hours pass. The TV won't pick up a signal, and there's no wifi — the only internet access is via a computer in the captain's office. I'd like a walk, see what's what on the ship, but Bernardo said to stay put, and I don't want to piss off the crew at least until we've set sail and it's too late for them to kick me off. Noon passes, and still I wait. So much of travel is waiting, watching the clock: tick-tock, tick-tock, tick-tock ...

After six hours idle in my room, I get a call on the in-room phone and am told to go to an office to meet the captain: a German in his late-fifties named Waldemar Murawski. I like that name; it's strong-sounding, seaworthy. I wouldn't be happy with a captain called Malcolm Shufflebottom. I'd trust Malcolm Shufflebottom to drive a bus, but not a cargo ship. "Welcome aboard, Herr Walters," he says as he crushes my fingers with his handshake. He tells me I'm free to go wherever I want on the ship. "You must be careful, though," he adds. "There are many ways you can injure yourself. You can fall over things; things can fall on you. And if you fall into the sea, it's a major problem — for us, and for you, but more for you." Then he gives me an indemnity form to sign; it says that I give up my rights to make any claims against the shipping company, even if they've been negligent. I ask if I can help out, put in a shift with a spanner, but he says no, I'm not allowed to legally; it would void their insurance if I screw up. For the best, really, as I'm useless with a spanner or, indeed, with anything practical. If I can't copy-paste something, and if there's not a delete button, it's better to leave it to someone else.

Back to my room, again waiting; then sirens sound: abandon ship — a drill. As instructed in the information booklet, I grab the life jacket and hard hat and head to the port-side lifeboat. I'm first there and feel smug to be. Ten minutes later, I feel less smug: a spectacled mechanic comes to get me to take me to the other side of the ship. I've been stood at the starboard-side lifeboat. Not my only faux-pas: I've come in a t-shirt and flip-flops, like I'm off to the beach. "You must wear a jumper," I'm told — told off, in fact, by the second-in-command, the chief officer. "It's cold at sea, *ja*?"

"*Ja*," I agree, speaking German as well as I can.

"And flip-flops, no. Trainers, you must wear trainers when you are out on deck. It's dangerous at sea, *ja*?"

"*Ja*. But, err, I don't have any."

He frowns and shakes his head, gives me the look one

gives a child who's eating crayons. "Then you will have to borrow trainers, *ja*?"

All the crew are here. The officers, engineers, and mechanics are German (except for Filipino Bernardo); the deckhands — those that do the hard, dirty work — are Kiribatian. I've never before heard of Kiribati, and it sounds as made up as Narnia. I'm told it's an island nation in the middle of the Pacific Ocean, and as there's no wifi, I'll have to take their word for it.

A few crew get in the lifeboat, lower it down to the water, and circle around for a while. As that's happening, I speak to the spectacled mechanic — a veteran; forty-six years on ships. He says 24/7 he's responsible for fixing anything and everything — big and small, from the engine to the toilets. He works for 3 to 4 months, then gets a month off to go home. He says this ship has gone from Europe to the US to South America to Africa to Australia, and after Singapore, will go to the Middle East.

I say, "Must be fun to get to see all those places."

"But all we get to see are the docks. We have to work the whole time the ship is at a port. We don't get time off to look around, go sightseeing or shopping or drinking."

I ask about pirates. "Around Africa — Somalia and Yemen — you're at risk?"

"We don't worry about pirates because of the speed of our ship."

"But they must have ships that are fast; surely speedboats?"

"Yes, they have fast boats — actually, faster than ours — but if the ship they're trying to board is moving quickly, it's difficult for them to get their ropes or ladders attached. And look how big our ship is; it's not easy to climb up here, especially if the captain keeps changing direction and speed."

"Guns, though; you have some? A few grenades?"

"No, we have none."

I guess they could improvise if they had to: use potatoes from the kitchen. While not as effective as a grenade, a well-aimed potato can cause a bruise.

Night falls, and we're still at port. Until, at 11 pm, a couple of tugboats latch on to the ship and pull us away from the dock. Then the ship's engine kicks in. I walk out onto the deck. A strong smell of oil in the air. With one hand, I hold onto a railing; with the other, I cling to my hard hat — it's so windy that it's at risk of blowing off. After fifteen minutes, we pass the lighthouse that marks the end of the harbour, and we're out at sea and soon rolling and pitching.

Back in my room, the wardrobe flies open, and my shower gel falls off its stand, and the curtains slide from side to side. As I lay in bed, I feel nauseous. The room spins like it does at the end of a night of too much boozing. The captain said many people get seasick during their first time at sea and that it can last for days. As I lay awake, awake and sick, I recap, again and again, what to do if we have to abandon the ship: grab the hard hat, the life jacket, a jumper; go down to A-Deck, turn right and go out the door at the end of the corridor, then go up one flight of stairs. I think: I could save some seconds if I sleep fully clothed. So I get out of bed and put them on, and while I'm up, put on the life jacket and hard hat as well — a few more saved seconds. Then I move from the bed to the sofa; nearer to the door — more seconds saved — and to lay against the swaying: instead of rolling side to side, my head and feet go up and down. It helps a little, but the creaks, cracks, and whirrs — that come from above and below, left and right — keep me awake, and I know I'm a prisoner to a sleepless night that will inch into dawn.

Swells in the sea — big ones — and still the ship rolls from side to side, but after a pep talk in the mirror — "Come on; you're a big boy, a big, big boy ..." — I don my hard hat and borrowed trainers and brave the deck. The ship's sides are too high for water to splash the deck, but the breaking waves make mist-like the air. The engine thrums, and I feel its might from below, and I hear the contents of containers sliding about. The barriers that border the ship's outer edge are only half a metre high, and the walkway is no more than a metre wide. I grip the rail — dirt and salt coat my hands — and nudge myself along at a pace only slightly quicker than stationary. "... a big boy ...," I remind myself, "... a big, big boy ...," for the ten minutes it takes me to reach the bow, where is an anchor — its chain as thick as my waist. After I sing *My Heart Will Go On*, I'm eager to return to my room, as I really could die out here: a big swell, a tumble over the side. The sea is unforgiving, merciless. In the outback, it at least takes days to die; in the sea, you could be doomed in minutes. It's claimed many more souls than the earth's deserts or mountains. To be lost and never found is probable. Which would be a bonus for my Dad — after the initial tears: "Well, he was the middle child, but we'll still miss him." — as he told me more than once before I left to make sure I have good travel insurance that covers shipping my body back, as it can cost up to £10,000. I ignored that and got cheap travel insurance (because it was cheap).

Back to my room to free my feet in flip-flops, then I head up to the "bridge" — the ship's cockpit. In it is a steering wheel thingy (not the official nautical name), a large control panel with hundreds of buttons and dials, and three monitors — two display radars and one a map. The map is super detailed; it shows not only where land is but sea depths and danger points. I see that we've detoured around an area marked "Explosives Dumping Ground". Bernardo is currently controlling the ship. He says he does two four-hour shifts here a day. If it's daytime, it's a one-man job, but they have two up here at night as there's a risk that a man alone may nod off. It's a risk because there's not all that much to do. He tells me: "It runs on autopilot except when near land or when passing through a congested shipping lane."

"Punch in the coordinates, then chill?"

He laughs. "Not exactly. We still need to watch out for other ships. And keep an eye on the speed — reduce it if there are large waves to prevent containers falling off or damage to the ship."

"How often does that happen? Containers falling off?"

"It's rare, but it does happen. At my previous company, we lost three tiers during a severe storm."

I leave Bernardo to go down for lunch in the officers' mess-room, where I eat all my meals. A waiter serves us food; he calls everyone "sir" — he calls me it too. He looks a bit shabby, with DIY turn-ups on his black trousers (each stitch large and white), but still, always good to be a "sir". Proper food, a full-time chef — a nice change from Australia, where for two months I survived on tins of beans and canned fruit, bags of nuts and Kit-Kats. Spaghetti today. Yesterday, we had Chicken curry; another day, mashed potato and chicken steak; beef and boiled potatoes, that we had too, as well as chilli con carne. We sit at four tables of four, with everyone in the same seat for each meal. Sit in near silence; barely a sound other than cutlery, hardly a murmur. They must run out of things to say after months of sitting next to each other for three meals a day — especially when they have no news or weekends to discuss. There are only so many times you can debate the best size and colour of shipping container before the topic gets dull.

"Herr Ernst, did you see the game last night?"

"No, Ulrich, I didn't. We're on a ship; there's no TV. I never see the game. You never see the game. No one on this ship ever sees the game."

"Ah, right, of course. So what did you do last night?"

"Nothing. I was with you. We both did nothing. We sat and talked about how we did nothing the night before. We had this same exact conversation — like we do every night."

"That's not true; not *every* night. There was that one night we were so bored that we—"

"We must never ever talk of that night. Never."

Later, land ahoy! We pass palmy coasts, tropical islands covered in jungle. Asia: to be precise, Indonesia. To the left, the island of Sumatra; to the right, Java. This the Sunda Strait that links the Indian Ocean to the Java Sea. And here the sea is calm, and its colour changed: from a dark blue to a soft blue-green.

I watch the scene from F-Deck (the top floor of the ship), sat on a deckchair, the sun on my face, the wind in my hair, and think: This is a moment, the sort of moment to travel for. I think too that probably these are the best days of my life, the days of this trip — days past, days to come. I know that now and don't need longing hindsight. Here, now: The dream being lived.

"I'm jealous," some say. "I wish I could do that." And I tell them they can. Then they say, "I will, but next year, or the year after. Before I'm forty, 100%. Fifty at the latest." But I know they won't.

Others say, "Mark, shouldn't you settle down? Get married? A house?" I hear that more and more since I turned thirty a year ago. Asked by boring bastards, that settling-down question often is; those chained to their town, their norm, to a career, getting a mortgage; those bouncing between an office and a sofa, saving, boozing, and shagging, stockpiling cushions and shoes. The "done thing" done, day after day. Shitty drudgery, fussing at the margins, suspended in a vegetative stupor; counting the empty hours down to 5 pm, to casual Fridays, to a weekend of prosecco and Netflix. Quietly stagnating while simultaneously frantically posting Facebook photos to prove the opposite.

I've opted out of that life, opted into this one — a life that's uncertain, but a life that's chosen, not just the done-thing-default. As soon as real-life came, as soon as I sensed that suffocating routine, I set off for a more breathable atmosphere. I went to Thailand, went to Korea, went beyond. I swam away from the mainstream, and I'm still at it — doggy-paddling my way to ... well, let's see where. Maybe I can't do this forever — on the seas, on open roads, without obligations nor responsibilities, no compromises nor constraints — but I can do it for now, press the pause button for reality until I'm forty at least. The way I see it, most people live until they're about eighty, and those years should be split between being settled and being unsettled. Eighty divided by two equals forty years of each. So it mathematically makes sense not to settle until you're forty. You can't argue with maths. To think you'll work hard when you're young, then go wild when you're retired, is bollocks. By the time people retire, they're mostly worn out; their vigour and enthusiasm wilted at best, died at worst.

Now I have my youth, my health, and diamonds they both are. I won't waste them on a hunt for riches and respectability — that's for sure. Freedom: that's what those diamonds will be spent on. Freedom to go here, to go there, to go anywhere; to wake up when I want to wake up, to eat a bowl of Coco-Pops at three in the afternoon; to quench my fancies, to explore the cracks of the world, to seek for the weird and wonderful, for novelty and for awe. Oh yes — sweet, glorious freedom.

And so on this bench, this bench on the MSC Uganda, the MSC Uganda cruising to Singapore, I'm glad I've left all that — the prison of routine, the humdrum ordinariness — left it for days clothed in uncertainty, to go mining for the extraordinary, digging deep; one day finding treasure, the next a dead body or a turd. And I will have my reward, so long as all I want are laughs and stories to tell.

Back to F-Deck at 6 pm for a barbecue. Most of the crew are here; the Kiribatians as well, but they keep to themselves, don't mix with the Germans. We eat steaks and sausages, baked potatoes, garlic bread, salad, beans. And drink beers, lots of beers — bought from the ship's shop, which opens for an hour a day. The shop sells beers (£9 for a crate of twenty-four Warsteiner bottles) and cigarettes (£7 for a 200-carton), as well as Ritter Sport chocolate and other foodstuffs from Germany — little tastes of home to see them through the long months away.

As we eat and drink, I ask the captain what he does with his free time on the ship.

He says, "I have no free time. I get email after email to deal with. It didn't use to be like this. Ten years ago, I'd get one lot of papers when I left a port, and that would be it until the next port when I'd get more. Now, because of these auto-pilot ships, they think I should deal with the stuff they used to do in their offices. When I was a child, my dream was to be a captain, but I never dreamed it would be like this: doing admin all day long. I don't want to work like this, but what can I do? It's the way the job is now. Not like when I started, when to be a captain you really had to know how to sail a ship, and you'd be at the bridge all day, sailing — *really* sailing. These days, the younger ones don't know much, don't know how to sail. If you took their tools away, they wouldn't know what to do. But they're good with computers, with spreadsheets, and that's what the shipping companies look for now. And they also want yes-men, guys who do what they're told. The reason for the delay at Fremantle was that I wanted more fuel before we departed, but head office said we had enough. There was only 250 tons of fuel put by for us, even though I told them a month ago that we need 350. I told them that to leave without 350 isn't safe. We argued, and, at last, they gave in, and I got the 100 extra. Who made that decision to say we need only 250 tons? Someone in an office who's never sailed these ships. Whereas I've sailed for decades, yet I still have to argue about stuff like that."

A week I've been on the ship. We may reach Singapore today, but I don't know. There are only so many times you can ask, "Are we nearly there yet?" — and I feel I've already exceeded that limit.

I've by now stopped looking out my windows: there's nothing to see but sea. The seven DVDs here I've watched: *The Matrix*, *The Matrix Reloaded*, *Enemy At The Gates*, and a few others. One day, I went to the gym, pool, and sauna. Once was enough. The sauna is the size of a fat man's coffin; the pool is a small metal box filled with seawater; the gym has only three pieces of antiquated weight-lifting equipment. To properly exercise, the only option is to run in circles — small circles because there's no space to run in large ones. The crew go months at a time without any decent exercise, which (along with the stodgy food) explains the chunky bellies. They get paid well and aren't stressed or overworked — just eight hours a day they do — but the boredom must take its toll. Every day the same, just ticking them off until they can go home. It's a cooped-up existence and one I'd struggle with. For me, to be on board is a novelty, but a week is plenty to play at being a sailor. I'll be glad to be back on terra firma, where I can run in circles as large as I like.

At 1.30 am, an alarm sounds, then the phone in my room rings: the captain says a Singaporean immigration officer is on board and wants to see me. The officer stamps me into the country without asking any questions — like: "Why the heck are you arriving on a cargo ship?!" A local aboard selling sim cards to the crew says he'll drive me into the city for £18. *Do I like the look of this man?* No. *Would I leave him alone with my sister?* No. *Is he the only way for me to get out of here?* Yes. So I'll give him a go.

Soon after, I'm sat in a van with him — Tony Lee, he says his name is — weaving through Singapore's streets. There's nothing to fear when arriving late at night at a place unknown with no hotel booked. Most will know the word "hotel" even if they know little to no other English. As for guidebooks, they're for beginners; they're travel-by-numbers, a comfort blanket. And are out of date as well: even if it's the newest edition — *Updated for 2014!* — there's a two-year lag from researching to publishing, and a lot changes in a couple of years. The best places — hotels, restaurants, whatever — for today are those that will be in tomorrow's guidebooks. To find them, word of mouth is everything, suggestions from travellers, from locals — from Tony Lee.

It doesn't always work out, this wishful rolling of the dice. You hope for the best but also must brace yourself for the appalling — and appalling is what the Hawaii Hostel is, the place that Tony Lee drops me, a place that seemingly survives on those too weary to be fussy. The receptionist is asleep across the check-in desk. After I wake him, he takes me to an ill-lit rathole without windows. Stains on the walls, scuffs and smears. £25 it costs, but I take it. For one night, I can sleep anywhere. I lay on the sagging mattress and think: I've done it; I've made it to Asia.

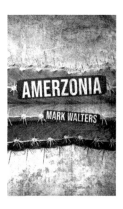

It starts in El Ceibo and ends in the Amazon; a savage journey in between, by bus and boat through Americas central and south. Along the way, a failed revolution, a spewing volcano, a drawer of cocaine; and a surreal assortment of oddballs and freaks.

www.gonzo.schule/amerzonia

EL CEIBO TO GUATEMALA CITY

A man the size of two men, biceps as thick as my neck. He's at a desk, on a chair large enough to be a throne, staring at me squirm on the sofa. My butt is sticky with sweat from the faux leather. His henchman, who forced me to come to this dingy room, is stood beside him, doubling the sullen eyes on the prey. Door closed. Blinds drawn.

"Pay," he says, his expression emotionless, the perfect poker face.

I say, "I'm not paying."

The more I protest, the less English he speaks, the more bullying his attitude. He soon speaks only Spanish.

I glance at the door: I could make a run for it. But the door may be locked, and I don't know where I can run to. I'm in the middle of nowhere, on the border between Mexico and Guatemala. And on the other side of the door are men with guns.

The room grows smaller with each second, slowly crushing my defiance. But I have some left: "I'm not paying," I say again.

He scowls, says, "*No pagas, no te vas.*" Don't pay, don't leave. Said with an absoluteness that permits no argument.

Gatekeeper is used as a metaphor; he's a literal one, in charge of this gate out of Mexico. He won't let me leave until I've paid £20 for a tourist permit. But I paid when I entered the country. He knows I've paid: it's impossible to enter Mexico without paying. Under the pretence of officialdom, I'm being mugged. He knows I know there's nothing I can do about it. He's the judge, the jury. If I continue to refuse, he'll tell me to sod off. It took me four hours to get here. To get to another border crossing, I'll have to return to Palenque and travel four-plus hours south from there — where I may have the same issue. Or he'll plant drugs on me. Not a sizeable amount — it wouldn't be believable for me to traffic against the northbound tsunami — but a gram or two he could get away with.

"Can I pay by card?" I ask.

"No."

"Can I get a receipt?"

"No."

I pay. I've no choice.

I call him a twunt as I'm leaving, wrapping it up with a Merry Christmas — "*Feliz Navidad*, you twunt." — to avoid suspicion. It's a safe insult, I think — surely he won't know that? Then I panic that he'll Google it, so I quick-walk off — as fast as I can go without running — past pickup trucks with

cargoes of people, past swindlers primed to sting: "*Señor!
Señor!*"

I got here — the border at El Ceibo — via a through-the-
night journey from Mexico City. Before boarding, airport-style
security: IDs checked and bodies frisked, luggage scanned
and searched. The driver locked in his cabin, the glass tinted
and bulletproof — shielded from bandits and the stink of
chow mein, which several passengers brought on board on
paper plates from a cafe at one stop. I had a seat next to the
bog; if we were ambushed, I could have used it as a panic
room. I'd have taken my chances, however, because the toilet
was vile, the toxic whiff like a soiled diaper on a warm day.
Drop-down screens with volume dialled to granny-friendly
prevented sleeping. Now, a battered minivan speeding along a
narrow, hole-studded highway to Flores in the north of
Guatemala. No one wears a seatbelt because there are none.
Trucks hurtle at us, thunder close by; the road barely wide
enough to squeeze in a couple of passing vehicles. Some cross
their chests, whisper prayers. They're right to do so: beside
the road are burnt-out chassis, victims of long-ago crashes.
Names of the dead are spelt in stones on the canvases
of hillsides.

The station at Flores is a frenetic jigsaw, its many pieces in
motion. Dust rises from wheels and footfall; people cover
their face, cough and splutter. Some spit, some piss on walls.
Shoeshiners struggle for silk purses from pigs' ears; the
shinees on wooden thrones, paupers playing princes. A guard
with a shotgun outside a shop — one selling day-to-day items,
not diamonds. Pilfer a pack of Oreos: BANG. You're dead. I've
no such protection. It's a sad state of affairs when you're worth
less than a pack of Oreos. Cries of "*Agua, agua. Fruta, fruta.*"
Others stick their head in minivans to peddle socks and
batteries, medicines and fireworks. Someone's selling a

framed picture of a woman posing sexily on all fours, a water-fall photoshopped in the background.

I board a minivan bound for Sayaxche, south of here on my screenshot of a map of Guatemala. The distance on the map isn't far, but the terrain between there and here is unknown. How long it will take, I've no idea: an hour or seven or twelve. I don't mind. Days like these on the road are some of the best on a trip like this; thinking and observing, channel-surfing, catching glimpses, flashes, bits. I'll ride until darkness draws down a veil, then bed down until sunrise. Where I don't know; I'll deal later with detail. No need to stress: always a town of some sort or size, always a hotel, a store. I won't sleep on the streets. I won't starve.

The van is buggered. One window cracked like a snowflake, stuck with sellotape. Strapped to the roof are soiled suitcases; also bicycles and sacks of all sorts, tied tenuously in place. My bag is on my lap. Any bigger and it would need to go on top, exposed to thieves, to the elements. It's the litmus test for those who say they travel light: if you're not comfortable with your bag on your lap for hours, it's not light. I have only 7 kg in my bag. I'm without all but the essentials — and also without several essentials: no towel, no trainers, no smartphone. (An iPod Touch is my only tech.) I have flip-flops and boots. A wise man packs hiking boots. A wise man I'm not: I've packed Chelsea boots.

Seats soon full. Plastic stools put in the aisle — soon full too. Several stand. One with a chicken; a live one, its feet and beak tied. Quetzales go out through windows; plates of tacos come in. Others buy fried slices of bananas or strawberries coated in chocolate. Crumbs tumble from mouths, adding to those already on the seats and floor. I'd pity the person who had to clean this van if such a person existed. We cruise about town with the door open, scouting for extras. Somehow squeezed in, another four children and three chickens. A butt nudges my face; a baby sucks a breast, close enough for me to suck the other. A girl sings Christmas-sounding songs. I'd prefer a Christmas-sounding silence. All but me are locals. My blue eyes give away that I'm not of this parish, that I'm a wanderer wandering, but no one's bothered about my presence.

I'm taking a locals' *colectivo* — rather than a tourist shuttle — to hide in plain sight. Desperadoes, I reason, are less likely to hijack a minivan of paupers than a busload of foreigners. Still, to be on the safe side, I have money stashed all over: various pockets and parts of my bag — even down my sock. A thief might empty my pockets and take my bag, but steal my socks, surely not. Paranoid? Maybe. But with reason: Guatemala is ranked as one of the twenty-five most dangerous countries in the world. It's fifth for gun-related deaths per 100,000 people. Police are overwhelmed: A force of 30,000 for a population of seventeen million. 90% of homicides remain unsolved. The past scars the present: endemic violence a legacy of the civil war that ravaged Guatemala from 1960 to 1996. Torturing, kidnapping, murdering. The police, the military, the government as guilty as anyone. At the end of the war, an amnesty was granted for even the worst crimes. No one was accountable.

As bad as it is in Guatemala, it's far worse in Honduras — twice the murder rate of Guatemala. And El Salvador — three times. I'll have to pass through one of those on my route south to the Amazon, where I'll go balls deep into the depths of the jungle to drink ayahuasca, a sacred tribal brew. William S. Burroughs — the original ayahuasca tourist in the 1950s — said it was the strongest substance he'd ever experienced. "It is like nothing else," he said. "This is not the chemical lift of C, the sexless, horribly sane stasis of junk, the vegetable nightmare of peyote, or the humorous silliness of weed ... This is insane overwhelming rape of the senses ... It is space-time travel ... You make migrations, incredible journeys ..."

Should I be in Guatemala? Should I be journeying overland to the Amazon through savage states so I can take the most powerful hallucinogenic known to man?

Yes. Dare to roll the dice, I say; risk a one for a six. And it's a story to tell. Life should be about stories. "So, anyway, this one time a narco shot me ..." What a shame, what a waste, to be sat in the old farts' home and have little to reminisce, be short on tales to tell.

"Grandpa," says Little Johnny, "tell me about your life."

"I worked in an office for fifty years. At weekends, I went shopping, I watched TV, I drank beer."

"Is that it?"

"Err, let me think ... oh, and I married your nan ... and nine years later, we divorced."

"Anything else?"

"No, that's all, basically."

"Oh," says Little Johnny, frowning. "Will my life be like that?"

"Your life, Little Johnny, will be different. You can be anything, do anything. If you want, you can be a pirate. A princess, if you prefer."

Then they hit eleven, start at big-boy school, and the bubble is popped. Dreams of being an astronaut are no longer tolerated. "Be an accountant, Little Johnny; that's where the money is, that's what pays the mortgage."

And so it starts: A lifetime of slaving and saving for a life that never gets lived.

Plus, it's worthwhile to disappear now and then, to go AWOL from reality for months: in your absence, friends and family remember only your finest qualities; they forget your faults, forgive your wrongs. It's almost as if you've died. On your return, the red carpet is rolled, and you're treated like the resurrection. But you have to disappear for at least half a year to places considered dangerous. A month in the Maldives won't do.

Out of Flores, a tropical landscape unblemished, as green and wild as Mother intended. The largest settlements barely stretch back from the road they straddle. Hardly a building is higher than a storey. Huts for homes, shacks for shops. Walls of wood; roofs of steel, of thatch. Some are concrete, bland and grey as the day they were built. Homes to be lived in, not looked at. To the residents, these communities are coloured and intricate, but what can I see in a passing second but that which is obvious, and what is obvious is poverty. It's more like India than Mexico. Mexico is more like the US than here. Breadline living, basic as can be, is the norm for Guatemalans: 55% live in poverty; 29% in extreme poverty, on less than £2 a day.

The road dead-ends at the bend of a river, the Rio de la Pasion. "Coban?" I ask the driver, the next town on the map.

He points over the river.

A motor canoe ferries me across. On the other side is Sayaxche, a town of dusty roads, of bumpkin commotion and bumbling disorder. Vans come and go; none set for Coban — their destination known via a sign in the windscreen or the shout of the driver. There's no ticket booth, no timetables. Purgatorial waiting ensues. It could be an hour, could be three. I may end up sleeping in Sayaxche. This is travel: A series of faltering transitions. Uncertainty is what you sign up for.

After a time, a driver breaks from yelling a destination that begins with R to ask me where I'm going.

"Coban," I tell him.

He doesn't understand.

I tell him again.

He still doesn't understand but tells me to get in the van.

I get in.

Coban doesn't begin with R, but I don't have to go to Coban. What is it to me but a strange name on a map? On this journey of long-distance aimlessness, wherever I am is where I'm meant to be. Each place is as worthy as any other. So on I go, on the move towards an uncertain destination, a destination that's only a destination until it's reached; then it becomes a departure.

After two hours, the van stops at a crossroads. The driver tells me to get out.

"Here?" I ask, gesturing at nothing. We're not in a town, not even a village.

"*Si*," he says, and more I don't comprehend.

I get out, hope the part I didn't understand was that vans to Coban, or to somewhere, will drive by, pick me up.

A van does soon come, from the direction the previous one sped off to. It stops for me. "Coban?" I ask.

He nods.

It's packed beyond capacity, of course, but I jump on board anyway, not wanting to chance getting stuck at this spot. This van also has a cracked window: the windscreen, the whole width of it. The interior panels are missing; the sliding door, at times, slides itself open. The only thing in good shape are the speakers — blasting eighties synth-pop. The driver's in a rush — they all are. He tries to overtake a truck on a bend, failing to see another oncoming at full throttle. Catastrophe narrowly avoided. He does the same again at the next bend.

This leg is on a remote stretch of road through Alta Verapaz, the greenest and wettest region in Guatemala, where on steep slopes sprout coffee and cardamon; through villages of indigenous communities where livestock wanders loose: flower-patterned blouses, flowing pleated skirts; babies stashed in slings on backs. Some sat like sages, stories written in their wrinkles; others at shacks, selling fruit. There a fellow riverside, panning for silver, perhaps gold. There one leading a donkey laden with firewood up a sinuous footpath to a lonesome building: a smoking chimney, holed linen strung on a line. The road rises and falls as it sweeps on through a densely-forested mountainscape — summits masked by mist. The rain just falls, the fierce downpour turning crater-sized potholes into swimming pools, and obscuring the driver's view; as does the steaming of the windows. With the rain, the steam, the crack, and the many stickers of Christ, he can see almost nothing.

Coban is drab, of no note; and Salama, the next stop, nondescript if you're generous, dreadful if you're not. A place to come to go, and the next place to go is the capital: Guatemala City. A bus this time, not a minivan; a so-called "chicken bus" to be precise: a decades-old school bus, a hand-me-down from Big Bro up north. At the end of their shelf life in the States, they're sent south for a new lease of life as a wackily-painted deathtrap. Besides a coat of paint, this one's jazzed with cuddly toys and a sound system that could hold its own in Ibiza. An eclectic playlist: sugary ballads to pulsing techno. Why bus drivers insist on playing dance-floor bangers, I don't know. No one on a bus wants to dance. What they spent on the sound system, they should have spent on the suspension: my organs are rearranged. These buses weren't designed to be driven at such speed. Haste to race ahead of other buses — to be first to pick up passengers — and also to thwart attacks: Gangs MS-13 and Barrio 18 govern here. To curb the gangs, there are police pickup trucks with swivel-mounted weaponry patrol; I saw them in Mexico, and I see them here: those aboard wearing combat gear, their faces masked with balaclavas.

The sun has set by the time I reach Guatemala City. A murder rate fifty times that of London. And even that is understated: The police don't count it as a homicide if a victim leaves the crime scene alive but later dies from the injuries. I want to hop on a bus to Antigua, 45 km away, but this is the northern bus terminal, and all the buses here go only north — where I've just come from. I ask at the information counter about hotels near the station. They say there are none, that I need to get a bus to the city centre. I board the bus they tell me to, the *Transurbano*; the others on board are mainly blokes, expressions chiselled to fuck-you. Outside, a teeming dystopia: Scummy suburbs sprawl, and on slopes are tacked dimly-lit shantytowns. Septic streets of chain-link fences and graffitied shutters, of scattered garbage and strewn liquor bottles. Heads pop up and peer, then quickly disappear, like urban whack-a-mole. Sinister weasels scuttle between cinder block boxes, skulk in the shadows. The discarded destitute fester: Rows of tents, ripped and stained, for block after bleak block; also dens and tarps and lean-tos, soiled mattresses and filthy, threadbare furniture.

Half an hour passes with me staring through the mucked window at signs that don't speak to me, thinking I can't get off here, or here, or here. I'm still hoping for a Starbucks or McDonald's — something that signals it's a safer spot than others — when the bus stops and everyone gets off. It's the last stop. No choice but to walk, but to where? Asking randoms where to go will show my hand, out me as lost and alone to them and anyone around. Fine in a rural town in the day, not in a homicide hotspot at night. So I stand on a corner and look up the four streets, assess which has the most life, and walk down that one. I do the same again, and again, and again, follow the flow of people, follow it past beat-up build-ings and glowering doorways and gutters choked with trash, past shops that have their fronts barred like cells, past scraggy mutts and scrawny children in scruffed clothes, their glassy eyes focused on the faraway. Hustlers and hawkers accost, alcoholics stagger and slur. Some curled up on flattened card-board boxes beneath boarded-up windows; some wrapped head-to-toe in blankets, looking like body bags. The vibe is gnarly, and I'm a beacon. The stares speak, but there are words too: "Faggot," someone shouts. Twice I'm asked for money; one moves his hand down the back of his jeans; a knife, an itch, I don't wait to find out: I run.

I see a hotel — Hotel Reforma — as shite as a hotel can be; I head for it. In the foyer is a waterless fountain; a Christmas tree, somehow wilted even though it's plastic. The room is a film set for a suicide. A lightbulb blinks sallow light on a grimed bedsheet, a 2009 calendar hangs. Television bolted down; toilet roll holder padlocked. Through papier-mâché walls: voices, music, horns, and the dull thud of a foot-ball being kicked — at one point, a hellish scream. Anything, though, at this time, will do. If all they had free was a dog basket in the backyard, I'd say, "Looks great; which corner do I crap in?"

mark@gonzo.schule

www.gonzo.schule

Printed in Great Britain
by Amazon

37606514R00121